TANNING LEATHER

FACILITATED,

BY

DAVID H. KENNEDY'S

PROCESS.

Engraved by J. C. Buttre

O. W. Kennedy

THE ART

OF

TANNING LEATHER;

BY

A NEW AND IMPROVED SYSTEM

THEORETICALLY AND PRACTICALLY

CONSIDERED IN ALL ITS DETAILS.

Discovered, and Patented April 14th, 1057.

BY

DAVID H. KENNEDY,

OF

NEW ALEXANDRIA, PENNSYLVANIA.

Illustrated with Twenty-five Wood Engravings and a Portrait of the Author.

Third Edition, with Additions.

NEW YORK:
BAKER & GODWIN, PRINTERS, NO. 1 SPRUCE STREET.
1857.

LETTERS PATENT GRANTED

IN

ENGLAND, IRELAND, WALES, THE CHANNEL ISLANDS
AND THE ISLE OF MAN,

On the 4th day of January, A. D. 1854.

FRANCE,

On the 20th day of February, A. D. 1854.

BELGIUM,

On the 27th day of April, A. D. 1854.

THE UNITED STATES OF AMERICA,

On the 14th day of April, A. D. 1857.

RUSSIA AND SPAIN APPLIED FOR.

BY

DAVID H. KENNEDY,

OF NEW ALEXANDRIA, PENNSYLVANIA.

These directions, when filled up, are not to be left exposed to the examination of such as may desire to possess themselves of their secrets. But should, for the benefit of the Patentee as well as the purchaser, be strictly kept from the public eye.

CONTENTS.

1*

PAGE.

CHAPTER VII.

CHAPTER VIII.

Composition No. 2.

CHAPTER IX.

Example.

CHAPTER X.

Example.

PAGE.

CHAPTER XI.

Example.

CHAPTER XII.

CHAPTER XIII.

CHAPTER XIV.

CHAPTER XV.

The Mechanics' True Position.

PREFACE.

The following directions have been prepared expressly for information as to the practical application of scientific principles which characterize the progress of the improvement, and are offered to that portion of the public which is interested in the leather and tanning business.

Like every other art, that of tanning has lately made great progress towards perfection. Ingenious and practical men have devoted their energies to actual experiments, and chemical agencies have been employed with varied success, until, at length, the desideratum seems to have been attained, which affords a new and complete substitute for the manufacturing of all kinds of leather. This must soon give it a world-wide celebrity, and entitle it to the attention of all concerned in the leather business. The Patentee, Mr. K., takes great pleasure in giving a comprehensive description of the different preparations for using the improvement; and I subscribe my hearty good wishes for the success of the invention for the purpose of procuring the desired information. Inquiries have been directed to the consultation of Sir Humphrey Davy, Professors Turner and Ure, and several other celebrated authors. In this way the author has obtained the most accurate knowledge of the chemistry of tanning, and for giving a full and comprehensive treatise on changing hides into leather.

CHAPTER I.

INTRODUCTION.

The art of tanning is that by which animal skins are converted into leather, a product differing entirely from that of the raw material, and adapting it to the useful purpose for which it is employed. The properties imparted are of a physical nature, and vary with the kind of skin employed and the modifications of the process which it undergoes. Chemically considered, however, leather is a definite compound of tannin and gelatin. Tanning, as an art, dates as far back as nine hundred years before Christ. The methods resorted to in early times consisted of little more than merely cleansing and drying the skins; and, thus prepared, the latter were used for clothing, &c. Leather was largely in use among the ancient Egyptians, and the workers of that material were so numerous that the Memnonian quarter, Thebes, was characterized as their especial locality. Their skill in fashioning it was so great that ornaments of all shapes and devices were made from it. Leather was made by them into tapestry, and many of the Egyptian tombs bear representations of artificers in leather engaged in the several branches of their vocation.

The principal steps in the manufacture of leather are the washing and soaking, for the purpose of cleaning and softening the skins, and preparing them for the removal of the hair. This is effected by the use of lime, or other substances which destroy, dissolve, or soften the bulbous roots of the hair, and thus facilitate its removal by mere mechanical scraping with a blunt-edged knife. During this part of the process, another important end is generally accomplished in the swelling of the tissues and their preparations for the more complete and easy absorption of the tanning principle. The primitive mode of removing the hair was that of shaving it off with a knife; but the use of lime was known even among the early Egyptians. When the rationale of depilation is better understood by practical tanners, the slow and inconvenient process of depilation by means of lime must give place to more effective, rapid, and economical methods. In later times, these defects were remedied by immersing the cleansed and de-haired skin in an infusion of oak bark or solution of alum, and thus, by effecting a union between one or more constituents of the liquor and a gelatinous tissue of the skin, producing a new compound with desirable properties. The principles governing this reaction have been, in more recent days, developed by the investigations of Proust, Deyeaux, McBride, and Sir Humphrey Davy; and it is owing to the researches of these inquirers that the occupation of the tanner has been elevated from the condition of an empirical pursuit to that of an art based upon scientific principles. Many improvements in the art have been made by the aid of ingeniously contrived machinery, and much has been done to hasten the process of tanning.

Tanning consists in the combination of

the gelatinous tissue with tannin by immersing the skins in an infusion of oak bark or other substances containing tannin. The tanning influence is probably not exerted solely by the tannin, but also partly by the extractive matter, more or less of which always exists in the tanning material.

During the soaking, the epidermis of the skins disappears, and the tissue of the latter is gelatinized, and thus predisposed to chemical union with the tannin. This gelatinization of the tissues is all-essential, and is promoted by the gallic acid fermentation of the tanning material. This is the more probable science. The same effect may be produced by the use of a very dilute acetic, and other operations intended to perfect the quality and appearance of the leather. Leather is employed for many useful and ornamental purposes; and numerous are its applications to various branches of industry. Besides its extensive use for covering the head and feet, wearing apparel, saddles, harness, carriages, and the purposes of the book-binder, it is largely employed for the embellishment of objects of taste and ornament. Independently of the direct importance of the leather trade, it exerts a very decided incidental influence in developing the resources of a country, by giving value to certain materials used in and resulting from its manufacture. Besides the immense employment which it gives to thousands of artisans, it has built up colonies and towns, which owe their origin and progress entirely to the interests connected with it. Even the waste materials of slaughter-houses, tanneries, curriers' shops and workers in leather, have important applications—the horns serving for the manufacture of combs, buttons, and umbrella furniture; the hair for plastering; the spent lime for the farmer; the skin-clippings for the glue-boiler; and the leather shavings for the manufacturer of prussiate of potash. The following statements will give an idea of the vast extent and rapid increase of the trade in leather.

In France—a country eminent for the quantity and quality of the leather which it produces—the average number of skins annually converted into leather is about three millions of whole skins, exclusive of sheep and calf skins. In the United States, the manufacture of leather is only beginning to be of much importance. Since the early part of the present century it has been rapidly extended, until it has become, with its allied and dependent arts, one of the most prominent elements of national prosperity. This improved system is conducted in the most simple and primitive manner. The expenditure both of time and labor is now materially reduced by the different modes and treatment of the process. The unparalleled success which has attended the introduction of the *patent* process set forth in this work, and the flattering encomiums bestowed upon the directions given in a former edition, induce me to extend them a little farther, hoping they will be understood by all those who will avail themselves of this improved system for the manufacture of leather.

I have extended the information in this, the third edition of directions, and hope that my fellow-tanners will read them with a generous allowance for the imperfect style in which they are given; hoping, also, that they will keep in mind that they are not fiction, but sober truths, intended expressly for the application of the process.

For some time past my whole time and attention have been given exclusively to the introduction of this process, believing from the first that its merits would, in time, bring it into general use, which is now acknowledged to be a fixed fact by those most conversant with it. Its general adoption is now only a question of time; for as fast as it becomes known it is adopted. This being the case, I wish to give all the information I can respecting the manner and different methods of using it. To those tanners who have adopted and seen fit to recommend this new process for tanning leather, I return my sincere thanks, and assure them that their kindness to me, and approbation of the improvement, will not be forgotten.

We append a statistical table, compiled from the returns of the seventh census, showing the condition of the tanning interest.

The National Intelligencer compiles, from the census returns, the following table of the tanneries in the United States, in A. D. 1850:

No. of establishments, . .	9,263
Capital invested, . . .	$18,900,557
Value of raw material, .	19,613,237
Value of product, . . .	32,861,796

The number of hides is 6,128,070; skins, 2,653,865; and about 6,000,000 sheep, goat, and other small skins tanned and dressed annually, which are not included in the number. The number of hands employed is 20,909 males and 102 females. The monthly wages of the males amount to $416,214; of the females, $970. The number of sides of leather produced annually, is 12,557,940, and of skins, 2,653,865.

The foregoing estimates were carefully compiled from the returns of the seventh census, for the National Intelligencer, and may be considered correct.

Leather forms one of the heaviest items among the staples of American merchandise, and the demands for it are daily increasing, in addition to its extensive employment for the embellishment of objects of taste and ornament.

If we take it for granted that the leather trade has advanced in amount at the rate of 10 per cent. per annum, for the last seven years, the figures should now stand thus:

Amount of capital invested, ...	$32,030,946 90
Value of raw material,	33,342,502 90
Value of product, . .	55,865,053 20

These calculations may fall short of, but it is believed that they do not exceed, the truth. They may at least serve to indicate the vast extent and rapid increase of the leather trade in this country. But what must it be a quarter of a century hence?

At the present rate of increase, we may fairly calculate that in twenty-five years hence the tanning and currying business will have TRIPLED, thus placing it almost in the van of all domestic manufactures. A business of such extent and importance, well deserves the attention of the manufacturer, for whatever abridges and facilitates the process, adds to the value of the capital invested.

The claims of this Patent are reasonable and philosophical. Tanning is wholly a chemical process, converting hides into leather. The perfection of the results of this process, depends not so much upon the energy and proper combination of such astringent properties and chemicals as are employed to effect it. The more rapid the action of these agents, and the quicker their work is done, the more perfect is the article manufactured. This is the doctrine of the improvement set forth in this work; and its correctness, economy, and great utility, we are ready to submit to the scrutiny of science and the test of the most thorough experiment.

The leather manufactured by this process is of a finer texture, softer, susceptible of a higher finish, less porous, more pliable, stronger, heavier, and more durable than leather tanned in the ordinary way. The quality of the material itself—which any man may examine—and its use and trial for years, authorize these high claims. They are announced to the public with the most implicit confidence in their accuracy and reliability.

We respectfully invite particular attention to the following statements:—

The numerous and great advantages of this improvement, both to the manufacturer and to the consumer, are matters on which the most satisfactory information may be obtained.

The adoption of this process by every tanner in the United States is practicable. It consists chiefly in the application of a proper compound or combination of certain chemicals to the usual bark, liquors or other astringent properties, possessing tannin, thereby causing a much more rapid advancement in the tanning of leather than is or can be produced by the ordinary process. It requires no new fixtures or expensive outlay. After the hides are tanned by this process, the scouring, stuffing, oiling, blackening, and finishing are conducted as they ever have been.

This improvement will be found of great general economy and utility. A correct knowledge of it must secure its universal adoption. The following facts sustain this conclusion:—Many of the most experienced, scientific, and enlightened tanners and other artisans connected with the manufacture or sale of leather, have certified to the superior excellence of the leather manufactured by this process, as possessing all the essential properties requisite for beauty and utility. We believe a similar opinion is entertained by all who have carefully examined the leather, and who are competent to form a correct judgment of the article manufactured.

To capitalists, and especially to those who have invested large amounts of money in the manufacture of leather, the following estimates, showing the difference in the expense of tanning, between the old method and this patent process of tanning, will be interesting:—

ONE YEAR'S WORK BY THE OLD METHOD.

To present this matter so as it may be readily comprehended by those doing a small business, we will exhibit it on a a small scale. Under the old method of tanning with bark, two men will tan and finish 4,000 sides of sole leather in one year. Their wages, at $30 per month, will be $720; the sides, in the raw and dry state, will weigh on an average, 11 lbs. per side, making 44,000 lbs.; at 32 cents per lb., they will cost $14,080; they will consume 270 cords of oak bark, at $7 per cord, making $1,890; rent of tan-yard, $150, interest on hides, $844 80; interest on bark,

$113 40; whole cost when finished, is $17,798 20. The 4,000 sides of leather will weigh on an average, 16 lbs. per side, making 64,000 lbs. At 32 cents per lb. they would bring $20,480, affording a net gain of $2,681 80 for one year's tanning on the old system.

ONE YEAR'S WORK BY THIS NEW PROCESS.

Under this patented improved system of tanning, ONE MAN will tan and finish 4,000 sides in one year. At $30 per month, his wages will be $360; the sides will weigh on an average in the raw and dry state, 11 lbs. per side, making 44,000 lbs.; at 32 cents per lb. they will cost $14,080; they will consume 135 cords of bark at $7 per cord, making $945, and chemicals to the amount of $600; rent of tan-yard, $150; the interest on the hides for six months, will be $422 40; the interest on the chemicals will be $18; the interest on the bark will be $28 35; making the whole cost of tanning 4,000 sides under this system, only $16,243 75. The weight of the 4,000 sides when finished, will be, on an average, 17 lbs. per side, making 68,000 lbs. of leather—a gain in weight of 4,000 lbs. over those tanned by the old method at 32 cents per lb.; —the whole would bring $21,760. The net gain is $5,516 25. Showing an advantage over the old method of tanning in one year, even on this limited scale, of $2,834 45; besides, the leather tanned by this process has a brighter color, more the appearance of oak-tanned leather, and commands a higher price in the market.

The above is a clear and accurate calculation of the cost of tanning, both with this process and the old method, and the result makes its own appeal to the good sense of all who are anywise interested in the profits arising from leather. Tanners! see you not that if so much can be saved by applying this patent process to tanning on so diminutive a scale, that the ratio of profit would be vastly increased by employing it on a more extended plan? You are invited to investigate this matter. If, on examination, you find that a substantial saving of even ten or fifteen per cent. can be made on a year's business by adopting this new process, you will not fail to see where your interest leads you; for ten per cent. over and above your accustomed profits would, in a few years, secure for you an independent fortune.

It is plain that the advantages of this mode of tanning, even to one who tans only sole leather on a small scale, are very great; and to those who find it difficult to obtain the usual quantity of bark, it will be invaluable. Where bark is plenty and can be obtained at a small cost, it also is valuable, for only one-half the usual quantity of bark will be found necessary. By adopting this method then, the tanner who consumes 1,000 cords of bark per year, will require only 500 cords; a saving at once of from $1,600 to $2,000 on bark alone, in one year.

A brief summary of the advantages of this patent process of tanning, may be stated thus:

Hides or skins can be tanned at much less expense than by the usual method. Common size calf, sheep, goat, deer, or other similar skins, can be tanned in from four to twelve days, at an expense of from fifty cents to one dollar and fifty cents per dozen. Heavier leather, such as kip, upper, bridle, skirting, harness, and sole leather, can be tanned in from twenty to ninety days, with a proportionate increase of expense, according to the thickness of the hide and strength of liquors used.

The liquors used in this process are in all cases applied to the hides or skins only in a cold state, and the leather manufactured by it has been found to possess more pliability, greater strength and durability, and a much larger increase of weight. It forms a finer texture, and gives it a handsomer bloom, and consequently finishes much better; thereby rendering it more impervious to water than leather tanned by the old method.

The whole process can be learned by any tanner in a very short time.

The apparatus and the different stages of the process of tanning, are the same or similar to the usual method; but capable, in fitting a new establishment, of being more compactly arranged, and at much less expense.

It requires less room or space to carry on the business.

Parties wishing to satisfy themselves on any point named in this or any other chapter of this work on which it is proper to give general information, are invited to call on the patentee or his agent, and examine the system in its practical operations, see the leather manufactured, and witness experiments which they are prepared to make at any time, for the purpose of illustrating and corroborating the claims of this patent, for which letters were granted on the 14th day of April, 1857.

NATIVES IN SEARCH OF WILD CATTLE IN THE TERRITORY OF BRAZIL.

CHAPTER II.

THE HIDES SUITABLE FOR TANNING.

THE hides and skins retain their original name until they have been subjected to the treatment of the various processes they have to undergo before they become leather. The quality of leather depends not only upon the nature of the skin and the mode of tanning it, but upon the result of numerous minor details, which require especial care and attention. Skins from large cattle are best, provided they are not thin and flabby, for such will make only inferior leather. Those from cattle slaughtered in the colder months give five per cent. more leather than hides taken in summer. The nature of the food and state of the animal's health, also, have an influence upon the quality of the hide. For the production of forty pounds of leather, there are required, on an average, twenty-five pounds of dry hide, fifty-six pounds of salted hide, or seventy pounds of marked hide.

SPANISH, OR WILD BULLOCK.

Buenos Ayres hides are taken from the wild cattle which are run down by hunters. After being removed from the carcass they are spread upon the ground, with the flesh side uppermost, and left exposed to the sun and air until dry. To prevent shrinking, the hides are kept stretched by means of wooden pegs driven through the corners into the earth.

One of these cattle, a Spanish bullock of the largest size, is before represented; and also the natives or hunters in search of wild cattle are represented by a wood engraving in front of this chapter.

Brazilian hides are nearly all slaughtered in the ordinary manner. It would be greatly to the interest of the tanner, and would save him much annoyance, if all hides were imported in a green state: that is, merely salted; for, when dry, it is very difficult even for the most experienced to detect many defects which would impair the quality of the leather into which they are to be converted. The large ox hides are the ones chiefly used for conversion into sole leather; for cow skins, though of denser structure, are rather too thin for this purpose, and are, therefore, reserved for making saddler's leather. This remark applies only to the hides of old cows that have repeatedly calved.

OLD COW.

These are weak and distended, but often tan well, and make good harness leather, and sometimes make a very good quality of upper leather. The hides of heifers, on the contrary, are equal, if not superior, to those of oxen.

Bull hides, on the other hand, are the least esteemed for making good leather, being thinner and more flabby than those of either oxen or cows.

AMERICAN FAT WORKING OX.

A well-fed, moderately-worked ox, when slaughtered in a healthy condition, will naturally yield a hide of normal quality; but if sick, lean, or deficient in hair at the time of being killed, then the hide is not adapted for making good leather. Should the animal die suddenly by accident, without being in a diseased condition, the quality of the hide is not thereby impaired. The hides from unhealthy bullocks or horses present a decided difference from those of the same animals slaughtered in a sound condition. This difference is not distinguishable by any very evident characteristic, though it seldom escapes the sagacity of an experienced tanner. There are no definite rules for estimating the quality of hides. If a skin is free from any defects, and has sufficient strength and thickness, with body and firmness, then it may be presumed that it will tan well and make good leather.

A skin presenting the opposite characteristics—that is, flabby, soft, thin, weak, and will not bear handling—should not be considered reliable. These signs, however, are not always unerring, for anomalous cases frequently occur. Indeed, it may sometimes happen that the hides from a diseased carcass, differing in appearance from the rest, will produce excellent leather.

As the skins could not be kept any length of time in a fresh state without being injured by putrefaction; and as it would be impossible to transfer them as soon as slaughtered to the tan vats, they are preserved unaltered by salting or drying them. The country butchers stretch them out in drying-lofts or in the shade, while those in the city generally salt them. In the sale of unsalted green hides there are certain reprehensible frauds which it is difficult to provide against. For instance, not only are the horns, ears, and other less valuable parts left upon the skin, but some butchers, in order still further to increase its weight, beds the animal before slaughtering in filth and mire, and then, after skinning it, trail the hide on the dusty ground.

Domestic, slaughtered, and heavy hides are converted into sole, belt, and harness leather. The very largest are selected and enameled for carriage tops. The smaller and lighter ones are used for skirting and bridle leather. In the old method they have to undergo a bleaching process, termed *fair finish*, which is avoided in this process of tanning. The smaller hides are sometimes converted into *upper*, and also for enameling and japanning, termed *patent leather*, when intended for shoes. The hides from the northern latitudes are preferable to those from the south. Hides from the extreme south are particularly objectionable for conversion into leather. Those from California, when free from the defects caused by unskillful skinning, are of good quality, and will tan well and make good leather.

SPANISH BULLOCK.

Spanish or South American dry hides are generally converted into sole leather and occasionally into belt leather. Those imported in the green and salted state are sometimes made into upper leather, which is of fair quality.

African hides from the west coast make good uppers; but they are largely used in their raw state for covering hair trunks. Madagascar hides are good when perfect, which is rarely the case, as they are liable to injury during curing transit.

The hides of the neat yearlings go into calf skins. Of these latter, there are "patna" kips, and common calf for bookbinders. The patna kips are very inferior, though frequently sold as "Calcutta kips."

CALCUTTA, OR NAGORE BULLOCK.

CALCUTTA OR NAGORE CATTLE.—These cattle grow to a very large size, and are used in India by the higher orders to draw their state carriages, and are much valued for their size, speed, and endurance, and sell at very high prices. They will travel, with a rider on their back, fifteen or sixteen hours a day, at the rate of six miles an hour. Their action is particularly fine. The Nagore cattle bring their hind legs under them in as straight a line as the horse. They are very active, and can clear a five-barred gate with the greatest ease.

Hides from Calcutta or Nagore cattle have the distinctive property of greater weight, and, when perfectly tanned, make a superior quality of leather. Tanners have undertaken to tan them, but failed in the experiment and pronounced the hides worthless.

I, at one time, for an experiment, tanned six dozen of Calcutta kip skins, in the space of fourteen days, by this process of tanning; and the leather produced was of a very handsome quality. They were pronounced to be a superior article of leather by some of the best judges and most experienced leather manufacturers. One dozen of those skins were taken to the State fair in Pennsylvania, and were awarded the first premium for being the best leather on exhibition. These kips sold at an advance price of fifteen per cent. in the Philadelphia market.

Hides from the largest of these cattle are best suited for making good leather, being strong and heavy, provided they have not undergone any injury during the importation.

A few kips come from South America, and some from England and Ireland. The supplies of the tanneries are mostly domestic skins.

CALF READY FOR SLAUGHTERING.

CALF SKINS are valued in proportion to their strength and size, and, when properly tanned, make excellent leather for boots and shoes, and also make superior patent japanned (termed patent calf skin) leather for fine wear. The skins of young calves are sometimes converted into parchment. The French tanners, who are renowned for the excellence of their calf leather, use the skins taken from animals of five or six months of age. Those from calves of less than two months old are very inferior, and only suitable for the manufacture of parchment.

Calf skins tanned by this process have superior advantages over those tanned by the old method. I have frequently heard gentlemen say they wore a pair of calf-skin boots on their feet which were manufactured from leather tanned by this process, and that they have worn them every day for a period of four months, without overshoes, and their feet have not been damp once, though they have repeatedly walked in the snow and sleet; and at present there is not the slightest appearance of cracking in the uppers, and the soles are apparently as good as the first day they put them on their feet. Calf-skins tanned by this process possess more strength, have a finer texture, and produce a handsomer grain; are more pliable and durable, and more impervious to moisture, than when tanned by the old method.

MUSTANG, OR WILD HORSE.

Horse Hides are tanned for uppers, and make good leather. They are also tanned for thongs, for sewing belts, &c., and are the best material for that purpose. Horse hides make good leather for japanning and enameling purposes; when well tanned and properly finished, make a superior leather for shoes and fancy mountings for ornaments of taste.

THE GOAT.

Goat Skins, when tanned and curried, are used for the uppers of ladies' shoes. Tanned in a particular manner and dyed with fancy colors, they constitute

Morocco or Turkey leather. The best goat skins come from Mexico, and are known in commerce as Tampico skins. The sound skins from the Cape of Good Hope are very large, and far superior to those from Madras and the Cape de Verds. Goat skins, when properly tanned and manufactured into good Morocco, make a superior leather for ladies' and gentlemen's wear, which is soft and pliable to the feet.

SHEEP AND LAMB.

Sheep Skins, when tanned in the old way, make a spongy, weak leather, used principally for lining and trunk trimmings. Saddlers and bookbinders also use them largely. When tanned by this process, they can be curried and blackened the same as calf skins; and they will make a very good leather for light shoes.

I have frequently tanned sheep skins by this process, and finished them in the same manner as true Morocco. The results of the many experiments prove to our fullest satisfaction, that sheep skins, when tanned and finished in this way, have many advantages over the old method of tanning leather: they are finer, more pliable and durable, and more impervious to moisture; and, when manufactured into boots and shoes for summer wear, they give full satisfaction to all who will give them a fair trial.

THE DEER.

Deer Skins, when tanned and finished in a proper manner, are used for the uppers of shoes; and, when finished in a particular way, make a superior leather for many purposes. By tawing, they are converted into chamois or wash leather, which is also made from goat skin.

Leather is differently designated in commerce, according to the use for which it is intended. For example: harness leather is blackened on the grain; russet is fair finished leather; wax leather is blackened on the flesh side; and buff is that with the grain divided by careful shaving, and blackened on the grain side. There are various methods of manufacturing patent leather which I will not describe minutely.

MODE OF SALTING HIDES.—This method consists in laying open the hide upon the ground and sprinkling the flesh sides with salt, more liberally at the edges and spinal portions than on other parts. They are then folded or doubled lengthwise down the center; the remaining folds are made over each other, commencing with the shank, then the peak of the belly upon the back, afterward the head upon the tail part, and the tail part upon the head; and lastly, by doubling the whole with a final fold and forming a square of one or two feet. This being done, they are then piled three and three together, and left until the salt has dissolved and penetrated their tissue, which generally requires two or three days. Thus prepared, they are sent to market. Skins may be dried, even after having been salted, by stretching them upon poles, with the flesh side uppermost, and exposing them to dry air in a shady place. Ten pounds of salt in summer, and somewhat less in winter, are requisite for each skin of ordinary size.

EXAMINING THE COMPOSITION OF THE SKIN.

CHAPTER III.

COMPOSITION OF THE SKIN.

THE skin of animals consists of an exterior covering, the *epidermis*, or *cuticle*, under which is a thin stratum of a peculiar substance, called by anatomists, *rete mucosum*, which lies immediately upon the *cutis corium dermis*, or true skin. The *epidermis* varies in thickness on different parts of the body; it is little prone to decomposition, insoluble in water, in alcohol, and dilute acids. Concentrated nitric and sulphuric acids soften and ultimately dissolve it. The caustic fixed alkalies dissolve it even when considerably diluted, but not the carbonated alkalies. It is stained by several substances, so far indelibly that the color remains till the cuticle peels off. It does not combine with tannin. Corns, and similar induration, resemble the epidermis in their general chemical characters; and horn, hoof, calves' feet, cows' heels, sheep's trotters, pigs' petitoes, nails, claws, tortoise shell, hair, wool, feathers, and scales may be regarded as modifications of it. All these substances partake more or less of the character of dry albumen, and Hatchett's researches have shown that the analogies between them are, in many cases, only broken by the presence of foreign substances. The general *color* of the surface of the body resides in the *rete mucosum*, the tint of which is much dependent upon the influence of light.

The black skin of the African, the brown of the Asiatic and American, and the pinkish-white of the European, derive their color from this peculiar secretion deposited between the *cutis* and *cuticle.* The nature of this substance has not been chemically investigated, but it has been ascertained, in regard to the black of the negro, that it admits of being bleached by chlorine. The *cutis* or true skin is of a fibrous texture, and, when boiled in water, is to a great extent soluble, leaving the vascular and nervous filaments which pervade it. The solution, when slowly evaporated, leaves gelatine, which is the principal and characteristic component of the *cutis.* The skins of animals consist of fibrine, gelatine, and small portions of albumen and fatty matter. The first two form, as it were, the basis or net-work of the whole tissue, a portion of which, if boiled with water, yields its gelatine, while the fibrine remains. The *epidermis* of the skin does not combine with tannin. The properties of these substances, which play such an important part in tanning, are as follows: Fibrine is one of the immediate and most abundant principles in animals. It exists in the chyle and blood, and is the basis of muscle; it is a white, tasteless, inodorous solid, heavier than water, soft, slightly elastic, and without action upon litmus. Fibrine loses four fifths of its weight by drying, and becomes yellowish, hard, and brittle, but regains much of its original appearance by soaking in water. It is insoluble in cold water, and hardens without dissolving in hot water, but is modified in its composition and properties. When left in contact with cold water for several days, decomposition, accompanied by a cheesey appearance, ensues. Dilute sulphuric acid shrivels flesh fibrine, and ultimately combines with it, forming a jelly soluble in water. Dry fibrine is changed by strong acid into a yellow, gelatinous mass, without being dissolved. If the acid be very dilute, the fibrine swells and becomes gelatinous. Concentrated acetic acid rapidly gelatinizes fibrine and renders it soluble in hot water. Tannin precipitates it from both its acid and alkaline solutions, and, when fresh fibrine is immersed in a solution of tannin, it becomes, on drying, tough, hard, and imputrescible. Gluten is the principal component of glue, and prepared in a pure state by soaking the latter repeatedly in quantities of fresh water until all soluble matters are removed, and by then boiling and straining the residue. Gelatine is colorless, or yellowish, transparent, tasteless, and inodorous.

It does not lose its transparency by drying, but becomes hard, brittle, and horny. It softens and swells, and very slightly dissolves in cold water, but is very soluble in hot water, from which alcohol precipitates it. Repeated and successive boiling and cooling of its aqueous solution impairs its gelatinizing property. The characteristic property of gelatine is that of combining with tannin and forming a grayish, glutinous, elastic compound, which, upon drying, becomes unalterable and imputrescible in water, and forms the basis of leather. The mutual affinity of these two substances is so strong that the latter will precipitate the former from a solution containing as little as one part in five thousand parts of water. Gelatine does not exist exactly as such in skins, and therefore leather, (a compound of gelatinous tissue and tannin,) though very analogous to, is not strictly identical with, this elastic precipitate of tanno-gelatine, which is slightly soluble in water, and becomes brittle on drying.

Mulder, who has examined the subject, says there are two definite compounds of tannin with gelatine. For example, when a solution of pure gelatine is mixed with one containing a great excess of tannin, the resulting precipitate, which is white and curdy, and becomes reddish-brown, hard, and brittle on drying, consists of one equivalent of tannic acid and one of gelatine. This is the neutral compound. If, however, the tannin be not added in excess, then the compound will contain three equivalents of gelatine and two of tannic acid. Earthy and metallic salts, throw down double compounds, one with acid and another with metallic oxide, the latter of which is wholly insoluble while the former is not entirely so. Tannin precipitates albuminous solutions, but the resulting compound is not softened by heat, like the tanno-gelatine.

Tannic acid combines with animal gelatine, forming an insoluble curdy precipitate. A piece of prepared skin introduced into a solution of tannic acid absorbs the acid and is converted into leather. A hide is composed of gluten. Leather and gluten are two very different and distinct substances. Leather is formed by a chemical action. The affinity of tannin and gluten is very great, and by the combination of these two substances we produce leather. This apparently compact mass of gluten, called green hide, is composed of millions of minute cellular fibres, interwoven and running in every conceivable direction, forming a strong network.

A VIEW OF THE HIDE-MILL, OR FULLING STOCKS AND THE WASHER.

CHAPTER IV.

WASHING AND SOAKING THE HIDES.

In order to prepare the raw hides for the action of the tanning materials, it is necessary to subject them to several preliminary operations. These consist in washing and soaking, liming or unhair-

Hide Mill or Fulling Stocks, and Washing Machine.—These machines are employed for the purpose of softening and washing the filthy matter from the hides, and thus, by bringing them as nearly as possible to the fresh state of the skins when first taken from the carcass, to facilitate the after process of depilation and tanning. The hides, with the hair on, are first soaked in cold water for twenty-four hours, or longer if necessary, and are then subjected to the action of the hide mill for an hour, which time is generally sufficient to render them pliable. Eight or

ing, and bating. Washing and soaking the hides is the first operation they must undergo, and it is therefore a great convenience to have the tannery located upon or near to a stream or running spring, with an abundance of water. The skins are taken in a green, dry, or salted state. The green hides are those from recently slaughtered animals. They are placed in the pool of water and left to soak for half a day, or longer if necessary, for the removal of blood and adhering dirt. If the skins are not very dirty, an hour is sufficient. If it should be necessary to soak them for a

---

twelve skins, according to their size and thickness, are generally put in the machine at once. A small stream of clean water is allowed to run into the apparatus upon the hides; and the washings, or dirty, filthy matter contained in them, is allowed to drain off at the bottom of the machine. This method of preparing the skins for the liming and tanning processes dispenses with the laborious manipulations to which they are commonly subjected, and preserves their quality—not injured as they were in the old way by the hands of the workmen. It also presents

longer time, they must be handled or moved about at frequent intervals. Dry hides necessarily require a longer soaking, and, to expedite the operation, it is necessary to remove them from the water and subject them to the fulling stocks or mill frequently. If there is no hide mill in the tannery, they must be stretched upon the wooden horse and scraped downwards with a fleshing knife. The fleshing should be repeated once or twice. The washing and scraping must be continued until all the slimy and other animal matters which are prone to putrefaction are removed. No definite

---

the additional advantage of not requiring a long exposure to the action of lime, which is so apt to injure their tissue. After the hides remain a sufficient length of time in the lime, the hair is removed by the workmen, and then subjected to the washing machine for the purpose of washing out the lime, which is accomplished in a very short space of time. The skins are then taken to the wooden horse and fleshed by the workmen. They are then placed in the hide mill and beaten in the same manner as before for an hour or so, washed and rinsed in a pool of clean water,

length of time can be prescribed for the soaking of the skins; they are to remain in the water until they have become supple, and the intelligence of the workman must determine when this point is attained. If this work is done by the aid of a fulling, or hide mill, as it is termed, it can be accomplished in one-tenth of both time and labor. If the soaking should be prolonged, the hides will acquire a tendency to putrefy. When the skins have been all soaked and washed as above directed, and are sufficiently supple, they are returned to and left in the water for a short time,

---

and then placed upon a truck car and conveyed to the tan pits, and there deposited in a weak solution of tannin liquor. A description of this machine, for the fulling of both small and large skins, is represented on the left end of the engraving in front of this chapter, giving an angle elevation. The trough in which the skins are placed is six feet long, three wide, and two deep in the clear, with a concave bottom. The end presents a quarter circle, against which the hides are beaten. The mallets or hammers are two and a half feet long on the under side, and

(five or six hours.) Some attention must always be given to the nature of the water, the size of the hides, and temperature of the atmosphere. It must be remembered that a too long continued soaking in the same water exposes the skins to the danger of putrefaction; and the rapidity of this decomposition is proportional to the amount of filthy, foreign matter contained in the water.

If the hides are subjected to the fulling stocks, or hide mill, as it is termed, and worked for a short time with judicious care, and having a small stream of clean soft water running in at

---

one and a half on the top side, one and a half feet deep, and one and a half thick, with grooved cast-iron plates fastened to each end of the mallets, supported by two upright levers ten feet long, the lower end mortised in the center of the hammers, and fastened at the top of the frame by a bolt of iron and wedges, so as to make the hammers perform their work correctly and prevent them from swaying out of place. The whole frame and size of the machine is twelve feet long, four feet wide, and ten feet high. The hide mill can be driven by water or steam

one end of the mill on the skins, while the dirty, filthy matter contained in them is washed out at the other end, skins thus treated can be softened and washed out completely in a very short time. This operation of treating the hides is represented by a wood engraving in front of this chapter. By this method, one man can cleanse a thousand hides in the short space of twelve hours.

The hides which have been well salted, but not dried, can be cleansed in a very short time in the same way as aforesaid. These manipulations are necessary not only for removing salt and

---

power. There are two pitments—the end of one being attached to the upright levers, about three feet from the bottom, and the other end attached to a cast-iron crank, each arm of the crank being ten inches in length, the two cranks forming a circle of about twenty inches in diameter, giving the mallets about a thirty-inch stroke upon the hides, driven at the rate of about eighty or one hundred strokes to the minute. A band or cog-wheel is attached to one end of the shaft when driven by power.

dirt, but also for rendering them soft and supple. When they are taken from the water for the last time, the rinsing must be vigorous and thorough.

Some manufacturers contend that the quality of the leather is improved in proportion to the duration of the time of soaking the skin. It is still undeniable that, when it exceeds a certain time, the skin acquires a tendency to decomposition, and the quality of the leather is thus impaired. It is a mooted point whether the nature of the water used for soaking has any influence upon the quality of the leather. From a

---

Washing Machine.—This machine is represented on the right end of the engraving. Its form and size are in the shape of a drum, five feet in diameter and six feet long, closed up at each end, with a trap-door in the front end for the purpose of passing the skins in and out. A pipe is so arranged in the center of the washer as to allow a small stream of clean water to pass in upon the hides, and small holes are made around the edge of the front end to let the dirty water pass out, with plugs to stop the holes

practical knowledge on this point, we will not take the affirmative side of the question. It is undeniable that the leather known as calf skin, upper, &c., and which, by its very nature and destined use, should be soft and supple, requires a soft, fresh, running water, and, consequently, that it will be difficult to make them so with hard water. Rain water is the purest, but all drinkable waters are applicable for tanning purposes. Tanneries that cannot obtain soft water can have the softness imparted to it by infiltrating it through spent tan. For this purpose there is a

---

and make the washer perfectly water-tight. The inside surface of the machine is set full of small wooden pins, one inch thick, about four inches long, and about four inches apart, for the purpose of catching the skins, raising them up, and, in falling, changes them in various positions. A six-inch wooden shaft placed through the center of the washer, set upon a frame erected for that purpose, with a cog-wheel and other gearing attached to it, so as to run the machine at the rate of twenty revolutions to the min-

series of three vats charged similarly with spent tan, and, as the water which is poured into the first vat is drawn through a cock at the bottom, it is transferred to the second, and, ultimately, to the third vat. In this manner all kinds of water may be rendered available for tanning, as, thus rectified, it contains a little tannin derived from the spent tan, which renders it particularly adapted for the early part of the tanning operation. Experience certainly proves the superiority of some waters over others for tanning purposes, but on what particular quality of the water this superi-

---

ute. If the washer is allowed to run any faster it will not do the work so well. When skins are tanned sufficiently to be skived, they are taken from the tan liquor and subjected to the machine for a short time, which washes them out completely. After skiving, they are again placed in the washer for a short time, which much facilitates and hastens the process of tanning.

Either of these machines will perform work much more rapidly and satisfactorily than any other machine now in

ority depends I have not yet been able to determine. The safest course is to prefer those waters which contain the least soluble matter, particularly earthy matters, for they certainly reduce the tanning power of the ooze by combining with some of its constituents.

---

existence, or than it was formerly done by the tedious and laborious processes practised in early days. The expense of building these machines is about thirty dollars each.

In the foreground of the engraving is the representation of a railroad and truck car loaded with hides. This road and car is for the purpose of conveying stock through to the different parts and places in the tannery. This, however, will be more fully explained hereafter.

THE BEAM-HOUSE—ILLUSTRATING THE MANNER OF HANDLING HIDES IN THE LIME VATS, BY PADDLE-WHEELS; ALSO, A VIEW OF THE SOAK AND WASH ROOM IN THE BACK GROUND.

CHAPTER V.

COMPOSITION FOR UNHAIRING.

THE second process to which hides are to be subjected is termed *unhairing*, and is that by which the pores are distended, the fibres swollen, and the hair loosened. These results are effected by means of alkaline or acid solutions, and by fermentation. Milk of lime is the

BEAM HOUSE.—This room comes next to the apartment for washing and soaking the hides. The beam house is the grand starting point for the manufacture of good leather. It depends entirely upon this operation for facilitating and hastening the process of tanning. To secure this desirable result they must be perfectly cleaned, scraped, and rinsed

alkaline liquor generally employed. Lime water has been proposed as a substitute, but it is less permanent in its action and requires frequent renewal in order to insure the perfect cleansing of the hides. After the hides have been sufficiently soaked, or, in other words, sufficiently prepared to receive limes or to be unhaired, I then introduce *Composition No.* 1 for the purpose of removing hair or wool, or for the purpose of liming, as it is called, instead of using lime as in the old way.

Lime has been used alone for the purpose of removing hair, wool, grease, mucus, and other impurities from the skins. Lime alone requires several

---

before being allowed to enter the handling house for the action of the tanning liquor. My tannery is two hundred and forty feet in length and forty feet in width, with a railroad running through the center from one end to the other. The room or apartment occupied for soaking, softening, and washing the hides comes first, and the next

days, and, in cold weather, weeks to effect these several objects; so that the muscular fibre of the hides is always more or less injured. When the composition is combined in proper proportions it modifies the action of the alkalies and protects the skins, so that the process of unhairing and liming are both rendered more expeditious, the hides are made much softer than by the old method of liming, their texture is uninjured, and, consequently, the leather is much stronger. The skins may be prepared for the bating and tanning processes after the usual method; but I prefer and use the following ingredients, which I shall denominate—

---

is the unhairing apartment. This latter operation and the apartment are represented by a wood engraving in front of this chapter. The center of the engraving represents a railroad, on which a truck car is coming in from the wash and soak room loaded with hides ready to receive the action of the lime. On the right end of the engraving

Composition No. 1.

1st, ...

2d, ...

3d, ...

This composition (No. 1) must be mixed in about the consistency of whitewash, with a sufficient quantity of water in the vat to immerse the number of hides proposed to be unhaired. The lime vats are placed along one side of the beam-house, each vat containing a paddle-wheel operating on the upper portion of the unhairing liquor, while the hides being handled are entirely loose and free in the vat, and move in

---

is represented five lime vats, with paddle-wheels for the purpose of handling the hides and agitating the unhairing liquor. The first wheel is represented as being in full motion, stirring up the liquor in place of the old tedious method of handling by hand. These lime pits are eight feet long, five feet wide, and six feet deep, with a concave

an opposite direction to that of the wheel. A gentle and yet effectual motion is given to the skins and liquor by means of the wheel. When the composition is prepared in the vat, the hides are thrown in and kept agitated at frequent intervals by running the wheels a few minutes at a time, say once every half hour, or once every two or three hours, as the case may require. This operation of unhairing the hides, and also the vats containing the wheels, are represented by a wood engraving in front of this chapter.

Although the management of process No. 1 is the same as the usual method, the skins must be handled or agitated,

---

bottom, for the purpose of making an easy revolution of the hides and liquor by the action of the wheels. These wheels are made in the form of the paddle-wheel used by steamboats, and are four and a half feet long, and five feet in diameter, or fifteen feet in circumference, each being geared independent of the other, with three cog-wheels, and closely attended to, as has been before observed. This composition for unhairing may be conducted at a temperature of summer heat, and the object may be accomplished much sooner than by any other process. One bushel of No. 1 mixture is about equivalent to one and a half bushels of good fresh-slacked lime.

The second ingredient may be substituted by eight pounds of ...., which will answer the same purpose. No. 1 process must be conducted with the greatest care and judgment, and should be kept at a mild temperature, and in a very short time the hides will be ready to unhair with-

---

two large wheels, and one small one. The small wheel is attached to an iron shaft running over the top of the paddle-wheels, with an iron lever attached to the small wheel for the purpose of sliding a clutch, by which the workman can run any of the wheels at the same time. On the left end of the engraving are four workmen represented at

out the least injury to the skins. After the hair is completely removed, the hides are put in the mill and milled a short time for the purpose of washing or cleaning them, which gives the skins thorough rinsing, and leaves them in a fine condition for the bate or the tanning process. I will add, according to my experience in unhairing and tanning, there are certain drawbacks in the liming process, when limed in the old way, which are worthy of enumeration.

Firstly, The contact of caustic lime alters, more or less, the texture of the hide, and permits it to penetrate the pores, and remain in them in the state of caustic lime or lime soap.

---

work, depriving the hides of their hair, standing upon a platform extending from the wall half over the pool, the whole platform being about ten feet wide, with the back end two feet higher than the front side, giving sufficient fall for the dirty water discharged from the skins to run off. The workman stands with his back to the pool, and

Secondly, The repeated rinsings in water and workings only partially remove the lime, which is a serious impediment to perfect tanning.

Thirdly, It hinders the ready penetration of the tanning liquor, and the perfect combination of tannin with the skin, and so obstinately resists removal during all the manipulation that a portion of it is found even in the best of leather. Notwithstanding that my experience is so opposed to the use of lime, the careful and elaborate experiments of Dr. Davy, chemist, show that its action upon animal textures generally is rather antiseptic than destructive. The disadvantages of the use of lime have led to

---

operates facing the light. In this position he can draw a hide from the pool and place it on the wooden horse, ready to be operated on, without moving from his truck, thus avoiding the old method of walking around the horse and drawing the hides up, which gives the workman double labor. After this manipulation is completed, the skins are

the substitution of less objectionable agents, which are set forth in this chapter. The advantages derived to hides by these substitutions for unhairing are superior to any other process, according to my judgment, and is acknowledged to be a fixed fact by all those who have used it. The skins immersed in this liquor swell out considerably, and are ready to be scraped in a very short time. Moreover, the alkali forming soluble soap, with the fatty portions, facilitates the cleansing and produces a smoother grained side than is done in the common way. Hides thus prepared will imbibe the tanning liquor more rapidly, and the entire processes can be accomplished in one-third of the usual time. After this

---

thrown upon the truck and taken to the fulling stocks and washer, and exposed to the action of those two machines for a short time. When thoroughly cleansed, they are again placed upon the truck and carried to the handling-house for the action of the tanning ooze.

mode of preparing the skins, they may be subjected to the tanning without additional process of bating, and there will be a firm, solid article produced. If the tanner wishes to make a soft, mild, and pliable leather, it must be subjected to the bate for a few hours, which will be set forth in the succeeding chapter.

CHAPTER VI.

BATING.

REDUCING THE HIDE TO ITS ORIGINAL THICKNESS.

These leading manipulations are modified to suit certain kinds of skins; and some undergo an additional treatment, termed bating, to remove lime and otherwise promote the thorough union of the tan material and gelatinous structure. The bate consists of a liquor made from the dung of domestic fowls; and immersions in this mixture remove the lime and reduce the skins to their original thickness. It acts by means of muriate of ammonia, which it contains.

This salt is decomposed by the unhairing process, which drives off its base, the ammonia, and, taking up with the muriatic acid, then becomes soluble muriate of lime, and passes off with the rinse water. When limed in the old way with lime alone, it carries with it at the same time a portion of the gelatine, rendered soluble by putrefaction of the organic matter of the bate, which undoubtedly occurs. If the hides are unhaired by the aid of composition No. 1, there will be no loss of gelatine in the application of the process; for, by bating, it will be entirely preserved from all putrefaction. The bating process can be conducted at the temperature of summer heat. This, however, must be attended to with the greatest care and judgment on the part of the workman, and will render the hides highly susceptible of being quickly tanned.

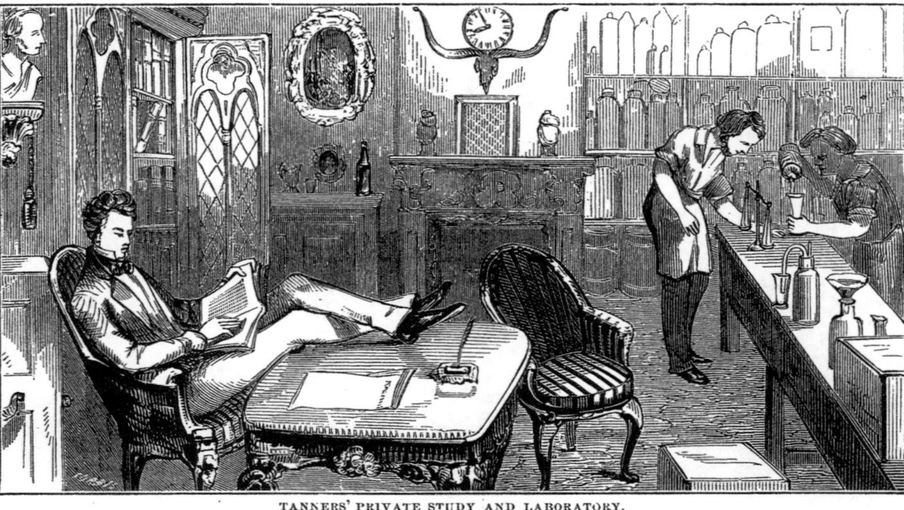

TANNERS' PRIVATE STUDY AND LABORATORY.

CHAPTER VII.

PROPERTIES OF THE INGREDIENTS EMPLOYED IN THE COMPOSITION FOR TANNING.

CHEMISTRY is that branch of natural knowledge which teaches us the properties of the elementary substances, and of their mutual combinations. It inquires into the laws which affect and into the powers which preside over their union; it examines the proportions in which they combine and the modes of separating them when combined, and endeavors to apply such knowledge to the explication of natural phenomena and to useful purposes in the different arts of life.

It is my intention, in this introductory chapter, to make a brief allusion to the style of these ingredients, used in this process for the manufacture of leather, when they are duly prepared in the proper proportions. The union of these ingredients with tannin facilitates the process of tanning, and produces the desired effect upon the article manufactured. There are many vegetable substances containing a principle which confers upon them an astringent taste, and which has the property of forming a superior tanning liquor.

Chemistry is that science which treats of those events or changes in natural bodies which are not accompanied by sensible motions. Most of the substances belonging to our globe are constantly undergoing alterations in sensible qualities, and one variety of matter becomes, as it were, transmuted into another. Such changes, whether natural or artificial, whether slowly or rapidly performed, are called chemical. Thus, the gradual and almost imperceptible decay of the leaves and branches of a fallen tree exposed to the atmosphere, and the rapid combustion of wood in our fires, are both chemical operations. The object of chemical philosophy is to ascertain the causes of all phenomena of this kind, and to discover the laws by which they are governed. As induction from experiment is exclusively the basis of chemical science, little progress could be made in it till the futility of the ancient philosophical systems had been shown and their influence annihilated, till the true end of science was rightly defined and the road to it rendered straight and passable, till the necessity of well-digested experiment had been established, which first procures the light, then shows the way by its means. The conversion of hides into leather is wholly a chemical process. Hides and skins may be converted into leather more perfectly by the combination of those different chemicals, ingredients, and tanning liquors manufactured from oak barks. By this combination a greater amount of tannin is concentrated in a smaller quantity of materials, and much less labor is required than in the old method. These ingredients, when combined in proper proportions, make a superior tanning agent for the manufacture of all kinds of leather. This composition consists of five different, distinct substances. In the succeeding chapter will be given a correct description of and the proper proportions for manufacturing and applying this composition to the hides. In the first place, as far as my knowledge will permit, I will endeavor to give the properties of the ingredients adapted to *Composition No.* 2, chapter viii., and their effects upon the hides and skins, and the purposes used for making the different kinds of leather. The tanner will observe that the ingredients are not all applied at the same time; but let him use them as directed, and he will not fail to produce the desired article of leather. Those ingredients are employed at different intervals and at different stages of the process of tanning:

Firstly, I use the first ingredient for the tanning properties it possesses. The tannin can be obtained from different sources. Its properties, however, differ materially in some of their characteristics. The tannin possessed by this article has superior tanning properties: one pound of it is equivalent to ten pounds of either oak or hemlock bark, besides containing pure tannin, and a small quantity of gallic acid and modified tannin, in the state which is generally designated by the name *Extractive;* and, lastly, a combination of tannin which is soluble in cold water, and more particularly in hot water, and produces a stronger liquor with the combination of chemicals, which unites dissimilar bodies into a uniform compound and makes a tanning liquor that cannot be surpassed. This article can be procured in abundance at the small price of from two to five dollars per one hundred pounds.

Secondly, I used the second article for

its brightening qualities. I do not, therefore, use it for any tanning properties, for it contains no tannin. It gives the leather that very bright hue which we term bloom, which makes a very handsome, durable, and saleable color. This ingredient is prepared on a large scale for calico printers. It has a cooling, saline, and bitter taste. When recently prepared it is beautifully transparent, but by exposure to the air it effloresces and the crystals become covered with an opaque white powder. By long exposure it undergoes complete efflorescence, and falls to powder with the loss of more than one-half its weight. It is soluble in three times its weight of cold water, and in its own weight of boiling water, but insoluble in alcohol; subjected to heat, it dissolves in its water of crystallization, then dries, and afterward, by the application of a red heat, melts, with the loss of fifty-five and a half per cent. of its weight. It has no injurious or offensive properties, for it was formerly used as a medicine. At the present time, immense quantities of this article are manufactured in all parts of the world, and can be procured at the small cost of one cent per pound.

Thirdly, I use the third article for the purpose herein set forth: it induces a more rapid action of the tannin upon the skin. This ingredient, when used in proper proportions, unites more forcibly, and adds materially to the quality of the leather, and makes it more pliant and durable, which is the great object in tanning.

This article is largely manufactured in all parts of the world, and is used for various purposes. Its cost is about six cents per pound, and it dissolves readily in boiling water.

JUST ARRIVED, A CARGO OF TANNING MATERIALS.

Fourthly, The fourth ingredient is used for softening the hides, and expediting the process of unhairing, and rendering them more supple for the tanning process, and also for keeping the skins in a fine condition while the tanning is going on, by keeping the pores open for the tannin to penetrate through the network of the hide, thus forming leather more perfectly and expeditiously. If the skins are hard and harsh, the harshness can be removed by the use of this article. It may be used freely without injuring the hides, as I have found it of essential use in raising the skins in the tanning process, and preparing them without injury for speedy and safe tanning. This article is manufactured on a very large scale both in Europe and America, and is used for various purposes. It has no injurious or offensive properties, and can be procured in abundance at one and three-quarter cents per pound, and dissolves readily in boiling water.

Fifthly, The fifth ingredient possesses a small portion of tannin, and also possesses a sweetish, astringent taste. Care must be taken and not use too mŭch at a time. When used too freely it gives the leather an olive hue, which is not a very desirable color. Its expanding properties are very great, and act freely upon the pores of the skin; therefore the proper proportions must be strictly observed, or the effects will undoubtedly be injurious to the leather. It dissolves in fourteen times its weight in cold water, and in its own weight of boiling water. It is manufactured in almost all parts of the world, and is used for various purposes, and can be obtained at two and a half cents per pound.

There are many other ingredients of similar properties that will answer very nearly the same purpose; but, upon experimenting with various kinds of chemicals, I could not find any that would answer for the tanning of leather but those I have adopted, and they answer the purpose in every respect. The reader will observe that the names of the ingredients are not given in this chapter, but they will be designated by being numbered in this and also in the succeeding chapters.

PREPARING THE DIFFERENT INGREDIENTS IN A COMPOSITION FOR TANNING LEATHER.

CHAPTER VIII.

COMPOSITION FOR TANNING.

This process is applicable to the tanning of all kinds of hides, and to making the different kinds of leather.

The proper proportions of the ingredients must be strictly observed in all cases. In preparing the following materials, the operator should use scales, and weigh them out correctly, as represented by the wood engraving in front of this chapter. Caution should always be observed to have the proper preparations. I will here give the correct proportions of the materials for the tanning of one hundred common-sized calf-skins, or any other like skins. The example of tanning the above skins will be given hereafter. In mixing these articles, the operator must be careful that he has the correct proportions, as it will depend entirely upon the management and skill of the workman in preparing these ingredients to produce a superior quality of leather, which will, undoubtedly, be the case when the process is correctly managed.

Composition No. 2.

1st, ... lbs. ....

....

2d, ... lbs. ....

3d, ... lbs. ....

4th, ... lbs. ....

5th, ... lbs. ....

The ingredients of number one must be dissolved, separately, in hot water; or, hot bark-liquor is preferable. After they are dissolved, put them into a vat or tub, or whatever it may be. If the liquor is not sufficient to cover the amount of skins proposed to be tanned, bark liquor may be used to fill up the vat or tub, to make the liquor cover the hides. There should, in all cases, be sufficient in, but not so as to lie crowded or in a compact state. The skins must have a sufficient quantity of liquor on them, so as to lie loose, and let the tannin have a chance to search through the network and fibres of the skins, which is one of the most important parts of tanning. When they are once plumped, we ought, at least, to keep them in that state, and allow them to come in contact with the tannin gradually, as they are frequently handled or agitated in the liquor. The spent liquor or water that remains in the pores of the hides, which has caused them to plump, by filling up every pore and cavity among the fibres of the skins, will retain its place, and will keep them in fine condition, just as they should be, until it is forced to give way to the tannin, which takes the place of the spent liquor, and gradually unites with the gelatin and forms leather. Hides should be handled in cold, weak liquor, particularly the first application of the skin to the liquor, for a day or two. The effects of the first application of liquor that is too strong, and too warm, to green hides is very injurious. It contracts the surface fibres of the skin, tanning at once the external layers so dead as to shut up the pores and prevent the tannin from penetrating the interior portions of the hide. This renders the leather harsh and brittle. The liquor should also be kept as cool as possible, with certain limits, but ought never to exceed a temperature of eighty degrees; in fact, a much lower temperature is the maximum point, if the liquor is very strong; too high a heat with a liquor too strongly charged with the tanning principle, being invariably injurious to the life and color of the leather. The first application of the liquor should not exceed, in strength,

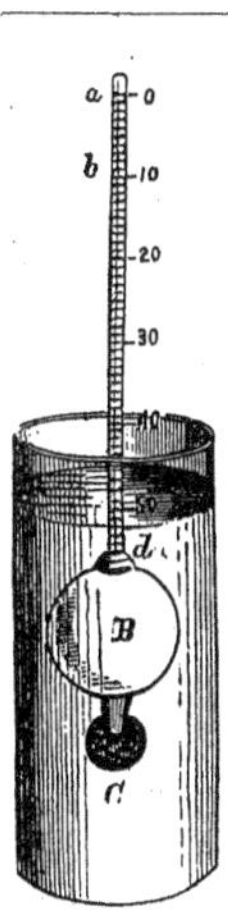

HYDROMETER.—A Hydrometer is a convenient apparatus for ascertaining readily the density or strength of liquors. That referred to above has been styled by its maker (W. Pike, of the city of New York), a Barkometer, because it is specially adapted to testing the strength of bark liquors. Its form and the manner of using it are represented by a small wood-engraving on this page; and it is made wholly of glass; *a*, *d*, being the stem, inclosing a graduated paper scale; *B*, a spherical bubble; and *C*, a small bubble at its base, containing quicksilver or shot, which serves as ballast to retain the instrument in a vertical position in the liquid. The scale on the stem is equally divided into

more than one or two per cent. by W. Pike's Barkometer, which is specially adapted to testing the strength of bark liquors. Strong liquor must invariably be avoided in the first application. On the other hand, a too weak solution, in the latter stage of tanning, must be avoided. In the latter stage, the liquor may be used as strong as it can be made, without injury to the leather. I have used it as high as fifty per cent. The weight, in leather, is made by keeping it in good strong liquor, and giving it close attention. In order to produce heavy weights, the hides should not be reduced too low in the beam-house, and should be tanned quickly, with good

---

five or ten wide spaces, and each of these again subdivided into ten narrow spaces; the zero point of the scale is made by plunging the instrument into distilled water, at 58 degrees F., and adding mercury to the bubble until it sinks to nearly the top of the stem *a*. A solution of ten parts of bark in ninety parts of distilled water having

strong liquors, particularly in the latter stage of the operation; green hides in particular. Nothing can be more injurious than to suffer them to remain too long in weak liquors. It will, from this, be seen that in the question of the proper strength of liquors alone, there is room for the exercise of the greatest judgment and the most extensive experience. In very many cases, nothing can be depended upon but the judgment of the practical tanner. In softening hides and preparing them for the process of tanning, a great deal also depends upon the judgment of the person superintending this operation; inasmuch as the diversities in the qualities and charac-

---

been made, the hydrometer is then plunged in the liquor, and the point to which it sinks therein, say *b*, is carefully and accurately marked upon the scale, and rated as 10 compared with the zero point. Each of the grand divisions, consequently, represents ten per cent. of bark, and each of the smaller ones, or subdivisions, corresponds with

teristics of the hides render it impossible to subject them to anything more than a general mode of treatment. As a general rule, the milder the process of preparing the hides for the liquor the better. Unnecessarily severe or prolonged treatment is inevitably attended with a loss of gelatin, and, consequently, with a loss of weight and strength in the leather. Skins should be handled in weak liquor at first; then increase the strength of the tanning liquor, and keep up the strength of it, and handle regularly, and of course the hides require less and less handling, as the process of tanning progresses—for the more they become tanned, the slower will

---

one per cent. of bark. It is very easy, therefore, after having determined the length of the stem from zero, which sinks in a normal solution of bark, to apportion the rest of it with the aid of a pair of dividers; so that every interval thus apportioned, shall be equal to that fixed by experiment. When, therefore, this instrument sinks into a

they receive the liquor; the hides that are intended for sole leather, when handled a short time, in weak liquor, should be laid down alternately in the vat, with layers of bark between each and every hide. (For example, see Chapter XI.)

When sole leather has been laid away for ten or fifteen days, the liquor should be let off, and a good strong liquor prepared and poured into the vat, without moving the hides, and let it remain until exhausted. The liquor should be renewed in like manner until the stock is completely tanned. The first liquor can be applied to a succeeding pack, and so on until the strength of the liquor is entirely exhausted.

---

bark liquor to twenty degrees, thirty, or any other degree, the number indicates the percentage of tanning force. It is necessary to observe that this instrument is applicable only to freshly-made liquors; for otherwise, confusion and want of confidence might ensue upon finding that it sinks, sometimes, to a corresponding degree in

The light stock, such as calf, sheep, and other like skins, need not be laid away. (For example, see Chap. IX.)

After the tannery becomes thoroughly impregnated with chemicals, it can be kept up with half the expense and trouble, and the tanner will see a great change in his leather, both in time and quality. No tanner should do without this process, if he looks to his own interest, which every tanner should do. If the stock is to be tanned out in a given time, it must be accomplished by management, care, attention, and strength of the liquor. It is my opinion that no practical tanner can fail in his appointed time for the completion of the work, if he closely follows the direction.

---

spent liquor. This is owing to the fact that the alterations which tanning liquors undergo during use and exposure, may not diminish their density, though they impair and destroy their tanning power.

EXPERIMENT OF TANNING ONE HUNDRED COMMON SIZED CALF SKINS, BY THE USE OF REVOLVING PADDLE-WHEELS.

CHAPTER IX.

EXAMPLE OF TANNING ONE HUNDRED COMMON-SIZED CALF SKINS.

The tanning of calf-skins is conducted about the same way as small cow-hides, or any other kind of hides. In the first place, the skins are subjected to a preparation liquor for the purpose of giving them a clear, bright color, and a good grain, and also for opening their pores and preparing them for the tannin. By this preparation mixture the skins can be colored and grained beautifully in the space of three hours. This mixture, however, need not be used in tanning regularly; only when you wish to color and grain the stock in a short time. It is more adapted to experimenting than regular tanning, although it is useful in tanning; but many tanners would think it rather troublesome to prepare. I procured one hundred common-sized calf-skins from the bate, unhaired and free of lime, and prepared a coloring and graining liquor of the following ingredients, which I shall denominate—

Preparation Liquor for Coloring and Graining the Skins.

1st, ... lbs. ....

2d, ... lbs. ....

3d, ... lbs. ....

4th, ... lbs. ....

5th, ... lbs. ....

I dissolve the first, second, and third

ingredients in hot water; then put the fifth ingredient in an earthen vessel—a crock—and put a little hot water in it; and then put the fourth ingredient in the latter vessel, and let them remain together until all were dissolved. After they were dissolved, which did not take more than ten minutes, I poured all the dissolved ingredients together into a vat, and put in a sufficient quantity of weak bark liquor to cover the amount of skins proposed to be tanned, then threw the skins into the preparation mixture. I handled them frequently for six hours. The same work has been accomplished in my tannery in the short period of three hours. At the expiration of the sixth hour the skins were removed out of the preparation mixture, completely colored and very handsomely grained. I then made a tanning liquor which I shall denominate—

(The ingredients in the following compositions will be recognized by numbers corresponding with those in Composition No. 2, Chapter VIII.)—

Composition No. 1.

.... lbs. of the 1st ingredient.
.... lbs. of the 2d ingredient.
.... lbs. of the 3d ingredient.
.... lb. of the 5th ingredient.

I dissolved these ingredients in hot water. After they were dissolved, (which took about ten minutes,) I poured them into a vat, and run in a small quantity of bark liquor, enough to make it cover the skins, and then threw the skins in, and let them remain in this Composition *number one* for twenty-four hours. The wheel was run about five minutes every half hour during the first day. At the expiration of the twenty-four hours, the skins were removed from Composition *number one*, and a new liquor prepared of the following ingredients, which I shall denominate—

COMPOSITION No. 2.

.... lbs. of the 1st ingredient.
.... lbs. of the 2d ingredient.
.... lbs. of the 3d ingredient.
.... lb. of the 5th ingredient.

These ingredients were dissolved the same as *number one;* and I added this Composition *number two* to *number one*, and strengthened it up. The liquor was well plunged up; then the skins were put in this composition for twenty-four hours; the wheel was run once every hour during the second day, about five minutes at a time. They may be handled by hand in the same way that many tanners handle their stock, which will answer a very good purpose for this process; but I prefer and use the wheel in all my handlings. In many tan neries they handle all their stock by hand, which is undoubtedly tedious, laborious, and very expensive; and, according to my judgment and experience, the leather is not as good and pliable as when handled by the wheels. The representation of tanning the aforesaid one hundred skins is shown by the wood engraving in front of this chapter. After the expiration of the second twenty-four hours, the skins were removed, and a new liquor made, which I shall denominate—

COMPOSITION No. 3.

.... lbs. of the 1st ingredient.
.... lbs. of the 2d ingredient.
.... lbs. of the 3d ingredient.
.... lb. of the 4th ingredient.
.... lb. of the 5th ingredient.

These ingredients I dissolved in hot bark liquor, then threw them all into the vat, as usual, and put in a sufficient quantity of middling good bark liquor to make it cover the skins. The liquor was well plunged up; the skins were thrown in and left remaining in Composition *number three* for forty-eight hours. The wheel was run about five minutes every two hours during the two days. At the expiration of that time I made a new liquor, and added it to *number three*, which I shall denominate—

COMPOSITION NO. 4.

.... lbs. of the 1st ingredient.
.... lbs. of the 2d ingredient.
.... lbs. of the 3d ingredient.
.... lb. of the 5th ingredient.

I dissolved these ingredients in the same way as *number three.* The skins were removed out of *number three*, and Composition *number four* added to *number three*, and plunged well up together; then the skins were put in, and kept in this liquor for two days. They were handled about three or four times each day during that time. At the end of the second day I had the skins taken out and green-shaved, which prepared them for the reception of the tan more freely than before; after which I prepared a new liquor of the following ingredients, which I shall denominate—

COMPOSITION No. 5.

.... lbs. of the 1st ingredient.
.... lbs. of the 2d ingredient.
.... lbs. of the 3d ingredient.
.... lb. of the 5th ingredient.

These ingredients I dissolved as usual, and put them in the vat, and added a sufficient quantity of good strong bark liquor, and plunged it well together; then put the skins in and let them remain in this liquor two days. They were handled about three or four times each day during that period. At the expiration of the two days, I had the skins removed and the liquor cast away. I then prepared a new liquor, which I shall denominate—

Composition No. 6.

.... lbs. of the 1st ingredient.
.... lbs. of the 2d ingredient.
.... lbs. of the 3d ingredient.
.... lb. of the 5th ingredient.

I dissolved these ingredients as usual; then threw them all together into the vat, and run in a sufficient quantity of good strong bark liquor, plunged it up well, and then put the skins in, and let them remain in this composition three days. They were handled about twice each day during that period. At the expiration of the three days, the skins were taken out perfectly tanned. The oiling, stuffing, blackening, and finishing is conducted in the same manner as when tanned in the old way. The skins tanned by this process possess different advantages over those tanned by the old method. They are finer, more pliable and durable, and more impervious to moisture, and, when handsomely finished, are equal to French calf-leather.

VIEW OF THE HANDLING HOUSE IN THE CLINTON TANNERY.

CHAPTER X.

EXAMPLE OF TANNING OX-HIDES FOR THE MANUFACTURE OF PATENT LEATHER.

THE tanning of hides for the manufacture of *patent leather* is conducted in the same way as the tanning of other

---

HANDLING-HOUSE.—The handling-house is the next place of operating upon the hides after they have been sufficiently prepared in the beam-house; for the manufacture of good leather a great deal depends upon the manipulation of preparing the hides in the beam-house. They should be well prepared before they are permitted to enter the handling-room for the action of the tanning principles. After the hides are deprived of their hair, and properly softened and rinsed in the beam-house, they are piled upon a truck car, and conveyed to the handling-house, and subjected to a weak solution of tanning liquor in vats, that are furnished with paddle-wheels for handling the hides

kinds of leather, with a little exception in the management of the tanning. This leather, known in commerce as patent leather, is very largely used for dress boots and shoes, and for fancy mountings. There are various methods of manufacturing it. I will here give an example of tanning thirty large ox-hides for japanning and enameling purposes. After they are unhaired and free of lime, or, in other words, well prepared for the tanner, we will subject the hides to the following composition, which I

---

and agitating the tanning liquors. The handling-house, as it is in Clinton tannery, is represented by a wood engraving in front of this chapter. A full view of this room is given by the illustration. The handling department occupies 26 feet in length by 40 in width; the right end of the engraving represents 5 vats, which are 8 feet long, 4 feet wide, and 6 feet deep—equivalent to 960 cubic feet of tanning room. Each of the vats is furnished with a revolving paddle-wheel; the wheels are 3 feet and 10 inches in length, and 5½ feet in diameter, or 17 feet in circumference; each wheel contains 11 paddles, 1 inch thick and 15 inches wide, and placed over the

shall denominate (see corresponding number, in Composition number two, Chapter VIII.)—

COMPOSITION No. 1.

.... lbs. of the 1st ingredient.

.... lbs. of the 2d ingredient.

.... lbs. of the 3d ingredient.

.... lb. of the 4th ingredient.

Dissolve these ingredients in hot water or hot bark liquor, whichever is the most convenient. After they are

---

center of the vat, so that the wheel dips 13 inches in the liquor; and the gearing is arranged to run the wheel at the rate of 18 revolutions to the minute. The center wheel is represented as in full motion: if they are permitted to run any faster they will not perform the work so well. The left end of the engraving represents 3 vats, which are 8 feet long, 7 feet wide, and 6 feet in depth—equivalent to 1008 cubic feet of tanning room; each vat is furnished with a handling-wheel, 6 feet 10 inches in length and 5½ feet in diameter, and placed on the vat the same as stated before. The first wheel is represented as being in motion. The illustration shows that each wheel is geared inde-

dissolved, pour them all together into the vat, and run in a sufficient quantity of weak bark liquor. Plunge it well up, and then throw in the hides. If the vat has a wheel in it, it should be run about five minutes every half-hour for the first day. I would let them remain in this liquor twenty-four hours. If the handler has no wheel in it, the hides must be handled up frequently the first day. At the expiration of the twenty-four hours, the stock must be removed,

---

pendent of each other by 3 cog-wheels, 1 small cog-wheel attached to an iron shaft running parallel over the top of the handling-wheels, with a pulley attached to the one end of it, and is forced around by a belt from the main shaft, running over head through the center of the tannery. By this main shaft all the works in the tannery are run. You will observe that a belt, running from this main shaft, is attached to a pulley connected with the pumps. The pump on the left side supplies the tannery with new liquors. The liquor is let off in the leaches, and runs unto this junk, to be pumped into the tan pits when required. The pump on the right side is used for pumping the old liquors up into the third story, and run into the leaches; it is first let off in the tan pit, and car-

and a new liquor prepared, which I shall denominate—

COMPOSITION NO. 2.

.... lbs. of the 1st ingredient.

.... lbs. of the 2d ingredient.

.... lbs. of the 3d ingredient.

.... lbs. of the 4th ingredient.

Dissolve these ingredients as usual, and pour them all together into the vat, and run in a sufficient quantity of bark liquor to cover the hides. Plunge it

---

ried into the junks by pipes or conductors, and then pumped into other vats or into the leaches for the manufacture of new liquors. The center of the engraving represents several workmen operating, and one man fetching a load of hides in, upon a truck-car, from the beam-house, ready for the action of the tanning ooze. The first application of the hides should be to a weak solution of tannin. No definite length of time can be fixed upon for running the wheels. If the hides are subjected to a liquor containing one per cent. of tannin, they should be run often at first; if the liquor is weak, they need not be run so often. The wheels should never be

well, and then throw in the stock and let it remain in this composition two days, and handle frequently each day. At the end of the two days, remove the hides and prepare a new liquor of the following proportions, which I shall denominate—

COMPOSITION No. 3.

.... lbs. of the 1st ingredient.
.... lbs. of the 2d ingredient.
.... lbs. of the 3d ingredient.
.... lbs. of the 4th ingredient.

---

allowed to run longer than 5 minutes at a time (less will do); they should be run once every half-hour, or once every 1 or 2 hours, as the case may require. The wheel must be geared for the face of it to move at the rate of 18 revolutions to the minute. Cog gearing has a decided advantage over belting, as the motion required is so slow that belts are often found troublesome. The motion wanted is slow and steady, which can be best had with gearing. It will be observed that a belt drives the shaft running lengthwise over the top of the paddle-wheels; and that each wheel is furnished with a pair of cog-wheels, and a pinion on the shaft above (which is loose), and is

Dissolve these ingredients the same as in the preceding compositions. After they are dissolved, pour them all together into the handler, and run in a sufficient quantity of bark liquor; plunge it well together, and throw in the stock, and let it remain in this liquor two days. Keep it well handled during that time. At the expiration of the two days, remove the hides and prepare a new liquor, which I shall denominate—

---

caught with a clutch, forced in or out with a small iron lever. These wheels are, of course, independent of each other. The pair of iron pulleys on the end of this shaft should be 24 inches diameter, and 6-inch turned face; the cog-wheels 24 to 26 inches diameter, 2½-inch face of cog, with pinion one-fourth the size. The shaft is, therefore, moving 4 times as fast as the paddle-wheels. It is seldom necessary to run more than 1 or 2 wheels at the same time; therefore a large number of wheels may be thus geared to the same driving-shaft, and with but one belt for the whole number. It will also be observed that they are plain paddle-wheels, operating on the upper portion

Composition No. 4.

.... lbs. of the 1st ingredient.

.... lbs. of the 2d ingredient.

.... lbs. of the 3d ingredient.

.... lbs. of the 4th ingredient.

Dissolve these ingredients as usual, and pour them into the handler, and run in a sufficient quantity of bark liquor; plunge it well, and then throw in the stock, and let it remain in this composition two days. If well fed and properly

---

of the liquor, while the stock being handled is *in the vats*, entirely *loose* and *free*, and moves in an opposite direction to that of the wheels. A gentle and yet effectual motion is given to the *stock* and liquor by means of the wheel, and a semi-circular (or semi-elliptical *lengthwise*) false bottom placed in the vats. This false bottom should be made with slats of inch-boards, 5 or 6 inches wide, an placed across the vats horizontally, and left about half an inch apart, so that the liquor under the slats, in the corners of the vats, will circulate among the hides, and so that the liquor may be drawn off while the stock remains in the vat. The wheel is placed *across* and over the cen-

managed, by this time it will be ready for splitting.

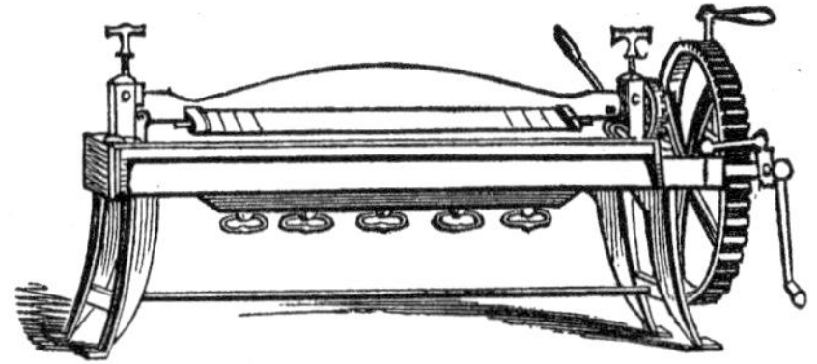

SPLITTING MACHINE.

The leather is sometimes prepared for splitting by being only partially dried. Hides that are intended for japanning and enameling purposes are generally split before they are wholly tanned, as

---

ter of the vat, and, when put in motion, will cause the stock to move up in front, pass under the wheel, and down on the back end of the vat, by the action of the floats of the handler; and a portion of the liquor urged by the motion against the slats at one end of the vat, finds its way between them and rises again between the slats of the opposite end, thus maintaining a constant circulation of the liquor throughout the vat. These handlers may be advantageously used for liming and bating, as well as tanning. The semi-cylindrical false bottom of slats, resting on the bottom of the vat, is an inch thick and 18 inches wide, the center of which is in the center of the vat,

the quality of the leather is thought to be improved by finishing the tanning after they have been thinned or divided by the machine.

After the hides are split, I would subject them to the following composition, which I shall denominate—

COMPOSITION No. 5.

.... lbs. of the 1st ingredient.
.... lbs. of the 3d ingredient.
.... lbs. of the 4th ingredient.

Dissolve these ingredients as usual,

---

planed on the upper side, and nailed to the vat; another piece is prepared with feather-edge slats, and nailed to the end of the vat, about half the way between the bottom and the top. The remainder of the false bottom is made in two parts, with slats placed half an inch apart, and with a space of about half an inch between each end and the sides of the vat. The lower part is fastened to the board with leather hinges, the upper part fastened to the end with a button. This arrangement is made that the vat may be cleaned when required. Care must be taken to have the false bottom, when in the vat, *level.* The vats may be three-fourths, or less, as deep as they are long,—

and pour them into the vat all together, and run in a sufficient quantity of bark liquor to cover the stock; plunge it well up, and then throw in the splits, and let them remain in this composition two or three days. Handle them often during that time.

If a soft, mild substance of leather is wanted, use the fifth ingredient freely. The second and fourth ingredients must not be used in this part of the tanning. At the expiration of the above time the

---

the lower part of the semi-cylinder, or false bottom of the slats, resting on or near the bottom of the vat. The false bottom should be made a half-circle, or a half-*ellipsis lengthwise*, and formed with slats of inch boards, about 6 inches wide, and placed in the vats horizontally, half an inch apart. The wheel should be two-thirds as large in diameter as is the diameter of the cylindrical bottom or the length of the vat. A vat 8 feet long may be 6 feet, or less, deep; and the wheel 5 feet 4 inches diameter; the diameter of the half-circle in the vat being 8 feet. A wheel of this size should have 10 paddles, as they should be about 18 inches apart on the outside of the wheel. Let the wheel be placed *directly over the center of the vat*, and

stock must be removed, and a new liquor prepared, which I shall denominate—

COMPOSITION No. 6.

.... lbs. of the 1st ingredient.

.... lbs. of the 3d ingredient.

.... lbs. of the 4th ingredient.

Dissolve these ingredients as usual, and pour them into the handler all together, and run in a sufficient quantity of bark liquor; plunge it well, and then throw in the stock. Let it remain in

---

the ends of the wheel must work within three-quarters of an inch of the side. The paddles should be made as wide as the wheel is intended to work in the vat; that will be about 2 inches wider than they are intended to be in the liquor. *The wheel must dip down 2 inches more than one-fifth part of the depth of the vat* after the false bottom is in. It is the most simple, effectual, and scientific mode of moving the leather in the liquor, and does away entirely with the necessity of handling by hand, facilitates the process of tanning to an astonishing degree, saves a great amount of labor, forms a handsome grain, and in all respects improves the quality and texture of the leather.

this composition until it is tanned; or, if this is not sufficient to tan it out, give them another liquor of the same kind, and tan them out. Leather tanned by this process, for japanning and enameling purposes, need not be subjected to the additional process of sumaching. The stock tanned by this process is whiter and brighter than any other tannage, and is more beautiful, finer, and more pliable.

TANNING SOLE LEATHER, AND LAYING IT AWAY WITH DUSTERS OF FINE GROUND BARK.

CHAPTER XI.

EXAMPLE OF TANNING FIFTY SIDES OF SOLE-LEATHER.

THE tanning of sole-leather by this process is conducted nearly in the same way as tanning with Spanish oak bark: only the tanning can be perfected in about one-fourth of the usual time, and at about half the expense, compared with the old method of tanning. Take twenty-five hides and prepare them for the tannin. In preparing, they are split or cut in half along the back, in a line from the head to the tail, making fifty sides. After having been well prepared for the tannin, I would subject them to the following composition, which I shall denominate—

(N. B.—The ingredients are recognized in the following compositions by numbers corresponding with those of Composition number one, Chapter VIII.)

COMPOSITION NO. 1.

.... lbs. of the 1st ingredient.
.... lbs. of the 2d ingredient.
.... lbs. of the 3d ingredient.
.... lb. of the 4th ingredient.
.... lb. of the 5th ingredient.

Dissolve these ingredients in hot water or hot bark liquor. After they are dissolved, pour them all together in a vat, and run in a sufficient quantity of the fifth run of bark liquor to make the liquor cover the amount of stock proposed to be tanned. Plunge the liquor up well, and then throw in the sides; let them remain in this liquor for two days. They should be handled once every hour during this time. On the first application of a hide to the ooze, I generally run the wheels once every half-hour, say about five minutes at a time, in order to keep the liquor and stock well agitated. At the expiration of two days, remove the stock and cast off the liquor. Then prepare a new liquor of the following proportions of ingredients, which I shall denominate—

Composition No. 2.

.... lbs. of the 1st ingredient.
.... lbs. of the 2d ingredient.
.... lbs. of the 3d ingredient.
.... lbs. of the 5th ingredient.

Dissolve these ingredients the same as before. After they are dissolved, pour them all together into the vat, and use a sufficient quantity of the fourth run of bark liquor to cover the stock in the vat; then throw in the sides, and let them remain in this liquor two days. They must be handled six or eight times each day during the two days. The first day, the wheel should be run about five minutes every hour; and about five minutes every two hours the second day. At the end of this period the stock must be removed, and a new liquor made of the following proportions of ingredients, which I shall denominate—

COMPOSITION No. 3.

.... lbs. of the 1st ingredient.
.... lbs. of the 2d ingredient.
.... lbs. of the 3d ingredient.
.... lb. of the 5th ingredient.

Dissolve these ingredients in hot

water or hot bark liquor, whichever is most convenient. After they are dissolved, put them all together in the vat; then fill the vat with third and half run of bark liquor; plunge it up well, then throw in the sides, and let them remain in this liquor for three days; handle about five times each day. At the end of the third day, the stock must be removed into a stronger liquor. The liquor of *number three* can be used for a succeeding pack, and a new liquor made of the following proportions for the first pack, which I shall denominate—

Composition No. 4.

.... lbs. of the 1st ingredient.
.... lbs. of the 2d ingredient.
.... lbs. of the 3d ingredient.
.... lb. of the 5th ingredient.

Dissolve these ingredients as before

described. When they are dissolved, put them all together in the vat; fill the vat with the third run of bark liquor; then throw in the sides, and let them remain in this liquor three days. Handle about four or five times each day. While the stock is green, it requires more attention than when nearly or about tanned. When about this stage, it absorbs the tannin very fast, and, consequently, requires more attention. Every tanner knows (if he don't, he should,) that when stock becomes nearly tanned it receives the tannin much slower than when in a green state. The liquor should never be allowed to remain on the stock after its strength is exhausted, for it will do more damage in one day than can be made up in four. At the end of the third day remove the sides. Use the old liquor for a pack not so far advanced, and make a new liquor, which I shall denominate—

COMPOSITION NO. 5.

.... lbs. of the 1st ingredient.
.... lbs. of the 2d ingredient.
.... lbs. of the 3d ingredient.
.... lb. of the 5th ingredient.

Dissolve these ingredients as is done in the preceding compositions. When they are dissolved, pour them all together into the vat, and run in a sufficient quantity of the second run of bark liquor. Plunge it well together, then throw in the stock, and let it remain in this liquor four days. Handle three or four times each day during that period. At the expiration of this time remove the sides; use the old liquor for a succeeding pack, and make a liquor, which I shall denominate—

Composition No. 6.

.... lbs. of the 1st ingredient.

.... lbs. of the 2d ingredient.

.... lbs. of the 3d ingredient.

.... lb. of the 5th ingredient.

Dissolve these ingredients in hot water or hot bark liquor. After they are dissolved, pour them all together into the vat; then run in a small quantity of the first and half run of bark liquor, and plunge it up well; and then lay the sides down spread out, lying or extending lengthwise of the vat, with dusters of fine ground bark between every side (what tanners generally term laying away), and let them lie in that condition four days without being moved or touched. A representation of laying down sides of leather alternately in a vat (what tanners generally term laying away) is shown by the wood engraving in front of this chapter. At the expiration of the four days, remove the stock. Use the old liquor for a pack not so far advanced in the tanning, and make a new liquor of the following proportions of ingredients, which I shall denominate—

COMPOSITION No. 7.

.... lbs. of the 1st ingredient.
.... lbs. of the 2d ingredient.
.... lbs. of the 3d ingredient.
.... lb. of the 5th ingredient.

Dissolve these ingredients the same as the preceding composition. After they are dissolved, pour them all together into the vat, and run in a sufficient quantity of the first run of bark liquor; then plunge it well together; and then lay the sides down with dusters, as described in Composition number six, and let them lie in that position five days.

In some tanneries they hang their stock across the middle of the side, in the vats, on slats running across the vat, with the butt and head down,—which is just as good for some kinds of stock as laying away. These ingredients may be used in the same way for hanging the stock in the vats, as for laying away, with the exception of using the ground bark when the sides are hung in the vats. The liquor must be kept up as the tanning advances. The liquor should be renewed seasonably, and its strength increased in a ratio proportionate to each stage of tanning. When five days expire, remove the sides, and prepare a new liquor, which I shall denominate—

COMPOSITION No. 8.

.... lbs. of the 1st ingredient.
.... lbs. of the 2d ingredient.
.... lbs. of the 3d ingredient.
.... lb. of the 5th ingredient.

Dissolve these ingredients in the same way as the former. After they are dissolved, pour them into the vat all together, and run in a sufficient quantity of very strong bark liquor; then plunge well up, and lay the stock down with dusters, as usual. Let them remain in that condition six days without being disturbed; at the end of the six days remove the sides. Use the old liquor for a succeeding pack, and prepare a new liquor of the following ingredients, which I shall denominate—

COMPOSITION No. 9.

.... lbs. of the 1st ingredient.
.... lbs. of the 2d ingredient.
.... lbs. of the 3d ingredient.
.... lb. of the 5th ingredient.

Dissolve these ingredients the same as in the preceding compositions. When they are dissolved, pour them all together into the vat; then run in a sufficient quantity of real strong bark liquor, and plunge it well up; then lay the sides down with dusters, as usual, and let them lie in that position seven days; at the expiration of that period take the stock up again, and prepare a new liquor, which I shall denominate—

COMPOSITION No. 10.

.... lbs. of the 1st ingredient.
.... lbs. of the 2d ingredient.
.... lbs. of the 3d ingredient.
.... lb. of the 5th ingredient.

Dissolve these ingredients as usual. After they are dissolved, pour them into the vat, and run in a sufficient quantity of real strong bark liquor; plunge well up; then lay the sides down with dusters of bark, as usual, and let them lie in that position eight days. At the expiration of that period, raise the stock out. Use the old liquor for a succeeding pack, and prepare a new liquor of the following ingredients, which I shall denominate—

COMPOSITION No. 11.

.... lbs. of the 1st ingredient.
.... lbs. of the 2d ingredient.
.... lbs. of the 3d ingredient.
.... lbs. of the 5th ingredient.

Dissolve these ingredients as usual, and pour them into the vat; run in a sufficient quantity of real strong bark liquor; plunge it well; then lay down the stock with dusters, as usual, and let it remain in that condition nine days. At the expiration of that period remove the sides, and prepare a new liquor, which I shall denominate—

COMPOSITION NO. 12.

.... lbs. of the 1st ingredient.
.... lbs. of the 2d ingredient.
.... lbs. of the 3d ingredient.
.... lbs. of the 5th ingredient.

Dissolve these ingredients as usual. After they are dissolved, pour them into the vat, and run in a sufficient quantity of bark liquor, as strong as it can be made. Plunge it well up, so that it will make a liquor about forty per cent. strong. Then lay the stock down in the vat, with dusters of fine ground bark between every side, and let them lie in that position ten days. This will make sixty-three days. The heaviest stock can be tanned in sixty days. I have frequently tanned sole-leather in forty days by the judicious use of strong liquors. Leather can be made as good in forty days as it can in twelve months.

Leather tanned in forty days is much heavier than that in the long tanning. When these ingredients are dissolved in good, hot, soft water, and mixed with good bark liquor, they will make a superior tanning agent, whose active principles are very soluble. By being gradually extracted, they will penetrate uniformly the whole of the animal fibres, instead of acting chiefly upon the surface, and will make a heavy, solid article of leather. In fact, one hundred pounds of dry hides, quickly tanned in good liquor made with this combination, will produce about one hundred and sixty-five pounds of sole-leather; while one hundred pounds of dry hides, slowly tanned in the old way, with bark liquor, produce only one hundred and forty-three pounds. The additional twenty-two pounds' weight in the quick tanning serve materially to swell the tanner's bill. At the end of ten days the stock may be taken out perfectly tanned, and, in less than three months, it may be finished and in market.

A VIEW OF THE CURRYING SHOP.—THE CURRIERS DRESSING AND FINISHING LEATHER.

CHAPTER XII.

CURRYING AND FINISHING LEATHER.

CURRIER.—The word currier means a dresser of leather. The derivation of the word currier is from the Latin,—the term for skin being *corium*. Both the ancients and the moderns have understood currying as the preparation of tanned skins for the purpose of imparting to them the necessary smoothness, color, lustre, and suppleness. Curried leather receives different designations, according to the modes of dressing it which are employed,—as tallowed leather, waxed leather, oiled leather, grained leather, and fair leather, &c.

The first operation of the currier is that of dipping the leather or softening it. For this purpose the skins are deposited in a tub containing water, standing alongside of the table, in which they are allowed to remain until they become sufficiently moist; or else they are sprinkled with water from a brush or broom, which is a much less effectual method.

SHAVING is the first operation of the currier. After dipping and softening the skins, they must be pared or shaved with a currying-knife for the purpose of securing uniformity of thickness and regularity of surface. When, however, the leather presents many weak and thin parts, this operation may sometimes be dispensed with or postponed until these have been filled up by the action of the stretching-iron. While preferences are given in different places to other modes of working some kinds of leather, all kinds, indifferently, are shaved by the currier. In some tanneries the skins are taken from the tan-pit, when about two-thirds tanned and shaved, to reduce the thick parts and let the tannin penetrate the skin uniformly. It is termed by some pating, and by others skiving. This operation, however, is dispensed with in many tanneries. The general plan or method of currying and dressing leather is about the same in principle, as in all countries they use oil, tallow, and labor, to make the leather suitable for the different manufactures to which it may be applied. The state of the leather at the time of their application has much to do with its quality and general appearance when the process of currying is completed. In many parts of *Europe* they want the leather perfectly saturated with oil, which they believe makes it more durable in wear. In *France*, they want a fine, light, soft, and mild article of leather, but not so deeply saturated with oil as to darken its color. In *England*, the public want a stout, heavy, solid article, no matter what the cost may be, as they find it cheaper in the end. In this country, we have a blending together of the whole, as our ruling principle is to get the most we can for our money. We find all grades, kinds, and qualities of leather at prices to suit the purchaser, while our best leather has ready sale, and is much sought for in the markets of Europe and Australia; and contracts for a constant supply of it are now matters of daily occurrence. Hence, we infer that we have facilities for obtaining materials. Science, skill, and capital are employed to an extent, in manufacturing all kinds of leather, that will ultimately command the markets of the world without fear of competition. A detailed plan of our mode of currying and dressing leather may not be understood by all, but I will endeavor to make it as plain as I can.

After the skins have been shaved, they are placed upon a marble table and the flesh side scoured out completely with a brush and clean water. After having thus been well worked, the flesh side is stretched upon the same table, and the hair side worked with a stone and slicker, and scoured to extend them thoroughly; the stretching-iron is then well laid on, by which process all the water is pressed out. The skins having in this way been freed from the greater portion of their watery contents, they may be held in readiness for the application of the oil. They then receive a light coat of oil on the grain or hair side, and are hung up by the hind shanks to stiffen or *sammey* (as it is termed), and are then exposed, for the purpose of drying, either in the open air or within the building,—one hour's exposure usually sufficing in summer, while in winter many more are required. After being sufficiently dried, they are taken down, and placed upon a marble table, and slicked out hard on the flesh side with a slicker or stretching-iron. After the skins have thus been well worked, they receive a mixture of oil and tallow, termed *dubbing*, upon the flesh side. After the skins have received their coating of dubbing upon the flesh side, and the workman has uniformly distributed it over the surface with the stuffing-cloth, he hangs them up by the hind quarters, and allows them to remain in the air long enough to absorb their contents of stuffing, taking care not to let them be exposed to the extreme heat of the sun or to a great draught of air, for, if they are dried too rapidly, the stuffing will not penetrate them in the gradual manner necessary for the perfection of the process. Twenty-four hours of exposure are usually sufficient in summer, while in winter two or three days are often required, according to the state of the weather. After the skins have become sufficiently dry, they are taken down, and the hair side placed upon a table, and the remaining dry stuffing removed from the flesh side by the slicker. They are then submitted to the action of the pommel, and are boarded up. These instruments are those best adapted for the purpose of giving flexibility and a granular appearance to the leather. The skin is first folded with its grain side in contact, then stretched out upon a table and rubbed strongly with the pommel, or *marguerite*, each quarter being made to slide under the instrument, over the leather below it, first toward the center, and then back to its original position. This mode of working leather makes it extremely flexible. To give the proper grain, the skin is then stretched out upon the flesh side, and pommeled from head to tail and crosswise. After the aforesaid process is completed, the skins are then taken to the beam or table and whitened. This operation is performed by some with the currying knife, on the beam; and, by others, the skin is stretched out upon a table, with the grain side lying upon a piece of smooth leather, fastened to the table, so that the skin can be held by the workman and whitened with a whiting-slicker, an instrument made expressly for that purpose. The latter is more generally used than the former. The skins are trimmed off around the edges with a common knife, and then about two or three dozen are placed upon a table for the application of the blacking. The blacking composition is made of oil, tallow, and lampblack. The skins are now blacked while still upon the table, and are moistened before this operation if they have become too dry, as a certain degree of humidity is necessary to enable them to receive the color. For the purpose of blacking, a mop of wool or brush of horse-hair is dipped in the composition and the flesh side is thoroughly rubbed with it in every direction. After the skins have received a sufficient quantity of blacking, a *size* is prepared of equal parts of glue and tallow, made to the proper consistency, and applied upon the blacking with a hard brush. When sizing sets, apply the glass slicker over the surface, great care being taken to avoid scratching it, and a fine, bright finish will be produced. Gum Arabic, or flax-seed oil, or gum dragon may be used, which will also produce a fine, bright, hard finish.

HARNESS LEATHER is finished about the same as calf-skins, with a little exception. The side or hide, whichever it may be, when dry, is placed upon a table and properly moistened with chamber ley or sal soda. A blacking composition is prepared of copperas, iron rust, and bark liquor. The blacking is applied to the grain side. After the application of the blacking, the workman distributes a thin coat of hard tallow upon the blacked surface, which is well stoned in. When a fine article is desired, apply to the grain side, upon the blacking, a good coat of stuffing, and hang it up until dry; then take it down, place it upon a table, and slick off both the grain and flesh side, care being taken not to scratch the finished surface, and a handsome, smooth, and solid finish will be produced.

BLACKED BRIDLE is finished the same as harness leather.

RUSSET BRIDLE is shaved and scoured, and generally is washed with a solution of vitriol and water, care being taken not to have the solution too strong. When tanned in the old way, with bark alone, it must be subjected to a solution of sumach liquor about twelve hours. (This operation is entirely dispensed with when tanned by this process of tanning.) After being sumached, the leather is then dipped in a tub or vat containing a solution of sugar of lead and vitriol, mixed in proper consistency with a sufficient quantity of hot water.

The leather is plunged in and out until the color suits the taste of the workman; it is then hung up to *sammey*. When partly dry, the table is stuffed, and the side is placed upon the stuffing on the table, and well set out with a glass slicker, which leaves a smooth, solid surface. A little oxalic acid and water is then prepared and applied upon the grain with a brush (which must be done with care), and a bright russet leather will be produced.

HORSE LEATHER is finished in the same way as harness leather.

WAX LEATHER is finished the same as calf-skins.

GRAINED LEATHER is finished about the same as harness leather. That which is intended for shoes and boots, after it is shaved to a proper thickness, is pommeled or grained for the purpose of giving to the leather the desired finish, flexibility, and granular appearance.

This kind of leather is used chiefly by shoemakers for the uppers of large shoes or stoga boots, the hair side being placed out against the frost and storms, in the same way as Nature placed it upon the animal's body, for protection against the inclemency of the weather.

Patent Leather.—This leather, known in commerce as "Patent Leather," is very largely used for dress boots and shoes, and for fancy mountings. There are various methods of manufacturing it. Two distinct operations are resorted to in the manufacture of polished leather,—one of which is the preparation of the surface for receiving the varnish, and which is effected by closing the pores of the leather, and making a proper ground by repeatedly rubbing the surface with pulverulent substances, and incorporating them with it; and the other is the varnishing of the leather thus dressed with suitable brilliant and transparent materials. The bases or medium of the substance used for both these purposes is linseed oil, made drying by boiling with metallic oxides or salts, and reduced to a sirupy consistence by the prolonged action of heat. Five gallons of linseed oil are boiled with four pounds four and a half ounces of white lead, and the same quantity of litharge, each in a state of fine division, until it becomes of the consistence of thick sirup. This mixture is then intimately united with one of the ochres, or with powdered chalk, according to the fineness of the skins which are to be prepared, and is uniformly spread upon either side of the leather, and well worked into the pores with appropriate tools. The leather is dried, after the application of each coat, by hanging it up, or, what is better, laying it out upon frames or racks in the drying room. The success of the whole process depends very much upon the care with which the skins prepared with it have been selected, tanned, and curried.

AN EXAMINATION OF THE TEXTURE AND QUALITY OF LEATHER IN THE SALES ROOM OR STORE.

CHAPTER XIII.

THE TEXTURE AND QUALITY OF LEATHER.

LEATHER.—The manufacture of leather has been estimated as only *fourth* in importance among the national manufactures of Great Britain. Leather is the skin of animals so modified by chemical means as to have become unalterable by the external agents which tend to decompose it in its natural state. It is evident, from what has already been observed, that well-tanned leather is a homogeneous substance, entirely free from unchanged gelatin or fibrin; but if the articles used in its preparation have been deficient in tanning ingredients or otherwise wanting in quality; if the various processes have been imperfectly or carelessly performed; or if unforeseen accidents have occurred, the excellence of the leather is impaired; and this is generally to be discovered by making a section of it. Well-tanned leather exhibits, when cut, a shining surface and compact body, and is of a uniform color, except upon the hair side, and has a nutmeg appearance internally. Those signs are commonly looked for in the tail, the back, and the neck, which are the thickest parts of the skin. Badly made or inferior leather is commonly detected by its section being of a yellowish or blackish color, alternately with streaks of a black or whitish hue, and by its structure being loose and deficient in density and compactness;

and a number of other circumstances give to leather a spongy and loose texture, and render it deficient in the requisite color and durability. These defects are of such a nature that, when once tanned, the leather cannot be improved or restored to a better condition. Some hides are called horny,—parts of which, from want of proper softening, are dry and almost as hard as horn; and these are entirely unfit for shoe or boot leather, as the tan has not perfectly penetrated the hard parts. Others contain extremely minute perforations made by worms, which allow water to filter through, and render them useless for either sole-leather or carriage-tops. Many hides are injured by the butchers, who damage the flesh side by a reckless manner of skinning. These imperfections can only be remedied by shaving the surface down to a uniform thickness, at the risk of making the hide thin and weak. Shoemakers using sole-leather which has been made from hides damaged upon the hair side, either in depilating, in paring, or in rinsing them, should be careful to place the flesh side out; otherwise, as soon as the hair surface has become a little worn, the sole will become spongy and easily absorb moisture. A common mode of determining the quality of leather is to allow a drop of water to fall from the end of the finger upon the hair side, on a cut surface. If the drop preserves its circular form, and does not extend, the leather is supposed to be well tanned; while, if the water is soon absorbed, it is regarded as an evidence of its substance being spongy and badly prepared. It is believed by some that leather is improved in quality by age; and it is a common reproach against shoemakers that they make use of too fresh materials. Exposure for a certain length of time is, doubtless, advantageous; but leather is not improved by being kept longer than two years; and is apt, after that time, to diminish in weight,—making it necessary to store it in damp cellars. The resistance and durability of the leather made into soles of boots and shoes are much increased by their being laid aside for some time before being worn. The coloring of leather during the process of tanning arises from a dark brown substance, existing more or less in the infusions of tanning materials, and called, by Sir Humphrey Davy, apotheme. This sparingly soluble substance is generated by the oxidation of extractive matter, and is gradually formed when infusions of tanning materials are exposed to the air,—all the varieties of tannin being, to a certain extent, liable to this transformation. Hence it is that the uppermost hide of the vat, being the most exposed, is the most highly colored. This color, or *bloom*, as it is technically termed, varies somewhat with the kind of *tannin* employed and the treatment or management during the process of tanning. Leather tanned with materials containing the gall variety and ellagic acid, or the pure tannic acid of tannin, is bloomed much higher and handsomer than with any other coloring matter, and which cannot be obtained in bark liquor alone. The pale or bright bloom or color is the product of the decomposition of strong or weak tannin respectively employed. Weak liquor yields less bloom, and stronger more, being richer in tannin. When properly managed, the bloom attaches itself permanently to the animal tissue and forms a beautiful, saleable color. The fawn color is the favorite bloom. In this quick process, the tannin being exposed for a much shorter time, yields a richer bloom than by the old and lengthy methods of tanning. Consequently, as time is an important element in the formation of tanning, by this process we diminish time, labor, and expenses materially. The more expeditiously the different processes can be accomplished the better will be the quality of leather produced. It is considered, however, by some, that it may be tanned *too* rapidly to be good. A greater mistake never was entertained by any intelligent mind.

After the leather has received all the necessary operation of finishing, it is then placed in the sales-room or store for the examination of purchasers, who generally make a very close and accurate examination of its texture, tannage, and quality.

An examination of the texture and quality of leather, in the commission house or store room, is represented by a wood engraving in front of this chapter.

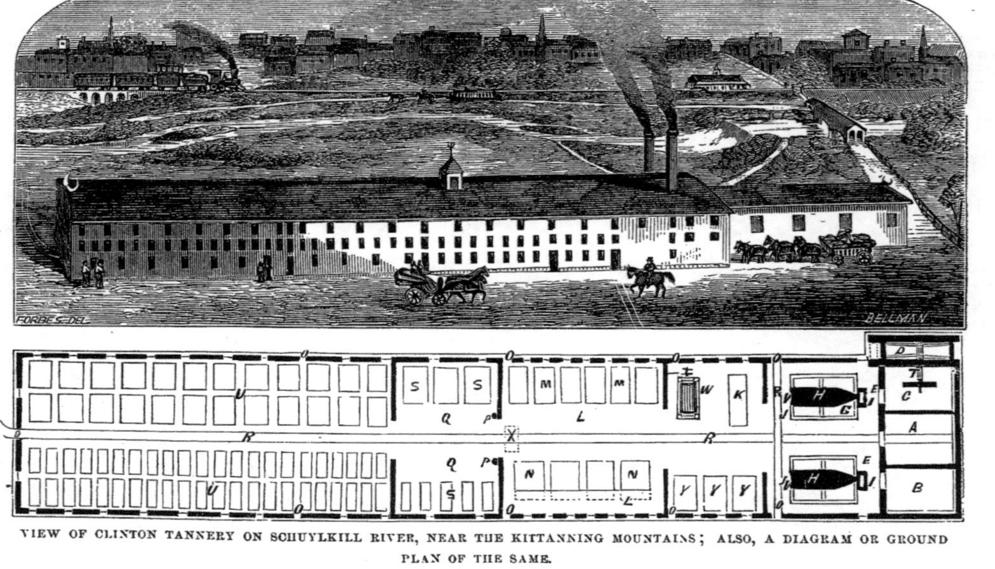

VIEW OF CLINTON TANNERY ON SCHUYLKILL RIVER, NEAR THE KITTANNING MOUNTAINS; ALSO, A DIAGRAM OR GROUND PLAN OF THE SAME.

CHAPTER XIV.

REMARKS ON TANNING.

The views I entertain and herein endeavor to express on this subject are the results of a practical experience in the manufacture of leather of various

* The Clinton Tannery.—In the old method, years ago, tanners were usually satisfied to locate their tanneries in the midst of a bark forest, upon a small spring, with merely a sufficient quantity of water for the manufacturing purposes, and work the machinery by the old and tedious process generally known as horse-power. The principles governing this reaction have been, in more recent days, developed by the most skillful and experienced manufacturers of leather. The combination of convenience and advantages derived from water-power—the readiness and cheapness with which bark may be ob-

kinds, and by very many experiments, prompted by a desire to improve in the manufacture of one of the first and most important articles of every-day consumption. Perhaps there is no branch of domestic manufacturing where there is so much room for, and need of, improvement, as in the tanning of leather. This country has been, and still is, overrun with patented *alleged* improvements in every branch of manufacturing business; and great improvements in almost every branch of manufacturing certainly have been made.

---

tained—has induced the tanner at once, without reflection, to locate upon Nature's elements, a place apparently formed for the designed purpose, and build a factory upon the most improved plan and of the largest size. The tannery is a wooden frame building, 240 feet in length, 40 feet in breadth, and 3 stories (each 8 feet high). Adjoining the north end of the tannery is a bark-house 90 feet long, 40 feet wide, and 16 feet high, with windows in each side, through which bark is received. Within the area of the tannery are contained 76 vats, affording about 15,652 cubic feet of room for tanning purposes, with sufficient

For the tanning business there have been but few patents granted which have proved useful; yet it will not do, in this age of progress, to condemn, untried, every new thing that may be offered. Let every alleged improvement rest entirely upon its own merits; for, whatever its merits may be, they will, in time, be known. We are too inquisitive a people to let true merit languish for want of encouragement. Perhaps no class of manufacturers has been so much humbugged by pretended improvements as tanners; for almost everything that

---

conductors for drawing the liquor to the pumps or junks—1 set under the bottom of the vats, and 1 within 3 inches of the top. Both set of conductors are connected with the junks, and also to the sewer or the waste-way, for the purpose of conveying off waste liquors and waters. Each of the junks are furnished with a pump of sufficient capacity to deliver all the necessary ooze charged with tannin. Eight of the aforesaid vats are arranged in the handling-house, furnished with paddle-wheels for handling stock; 3 of these are placed on one side and 5 on the other. The beam-house contains 13 vats—equivalent to

has been presented has utterly failed to answer the purposes pretended. Therefore it is quite necessary that the tanner be cautious in adopting anything new; for his business is one requiring a heavy outlay of capital, and any unfortunate experiment he may try may prove a serious loss. But if an improvement be made, and then fully proved and demonstrated—proved as represented—then the sooner the tanner avails himself of the advantage of it the better; for those who take hold of all good improvements in their business are those that are most successful.

4,098 cubic feet—for liming, bating, and soaking purposes. It has connected with it a hide-mill and washing-machine, for softening, washing, and cleansing the hides. There are 4 leaches—equivalent to 5,120 cubic feet of room—for extracting the tannin from bark for the tanning of hides, which are furnished with two copper heaters. The upper or north end of the tannery is built against a bank, making the second story on a level with the surface of the earth. Under the north-east corner (in the tannery connected with the beam-house) is a sweat pit (built of stone), ar-

There is yet, in my opinion, much to learn in the art and mystery of tanning. It is, to all intents and purposes, a chemical process, and requires much practical experience as well as mental research. What is tanning but a chemical operation from the beginning to the end—changing hides into leather? The manufacturing of leather, more than any other mechanical branch of business, is a chemical process, almost wholly relying upon the skill and judgment with which the principles of tanning are conducted. To attain the requisite skill in the

---

ranged upon the most approved plan. In the opposite corner, on the same level, is the machinery room, where the water-wheel is attached to the gearing for the purpose of running the different work in the factory. In the center, between these two rooms, is a room for depositing ground bark after falling from the bark-mill, which is placed on the second story. In this room, under the bark mill, are elevators, for carrying the ground bark up into the third story for the purpose of supplying the leaches. *See Diagram*, which is represented by a wood engraving in front of this chapter, and as *follows: A* is the bark-

laboratory of the chemist is evidently impossible. It can only be acquired in the tanning process itself by careful and close observation. The question has been frequently asked, How long does it take to tan sole-leather? By the old method of tanning, with bark alone, it takes from *eight* to *fifteen* months; by this system of tanning it takes from *two* to *three* months, according to the thickness of the sides, the strength of the liquor, and the number of sides in the vats; and the quicker tanned the better. I would here remark, that several con-

---

room, 20 feet in length, 13 feet in width, and 8 feet high, made very close, for containing fine ground bark as it falls from the bark-mill, and preserved until conveyed by a truck-car to the tan-pits for laying away the stock. *B* is a sweat pit, for sweating hides, which destroy, dissolve, or soften the bulbous roots of the hair in the place of lime, and thus the hair is removed; this room is built of stone, and is, in the area, 20 feet in length, 11 feet in width, and 8 feet in depth. *C* is the machinery department, 11 feet wide, 20 feet long, and 8 feet high. *D* is the water-wheel, placed on the north-west corner of the tannery, 20 feet in

siderations must be noticed in order to meet the questions understandingly.

First, I should say that the hides (as every one knows), if *heavy*, require more time than if comparatively *light*.

Second, If the hides are fresh, they are capable of being properly softened; and, if so, the process of tanning can be completed much sooner than in case of old and hard hides, that cannot be softened with the same facility.

Third, If the hides have sufficient room in the vat, so as not to lie crowded, they will tan much faster than when crowded.

---

diameter, and 8 feet wide, with an over-shot power equivalent to 50-horse power, driven by water brought from the Schuylkill River, in a race, from a dam made expressly for that purpose. *T* is the water-wheel shaft, extending from the wheel into the machinery-room, and there connected by gearing to the work in the tannery. *E* is an entrance to the sweat pit. *F* is an entrance to the machinery room. *G* is 4 leaches, each 16 feet in length, 8 feet in width, and 10 feet in depth; the 4 leaches will contain 5,120 cubic feet of bark and water for the manufac-

Fourth, As the tanning advances the liquor should be renewed seasonably, and its strength increased in a ratio proportionable to each stage of tanning.

Fifth, When the process of tanning is once commenced, it should not be allowed to cease until the stock is completely tanned; and, in order that the process may be continually going on, the stock requires a constant increase of the strength of the liquor.

Sixth, The question is, Is the leather to be tanned so as barely to pass in market, or to be well prepared, so as to make firm and solid leather? This

ture of tannin; the bottom of the leaches are 3 feet above the level of the top of the tan-pits, which makes them occupy the second story as well as the first; the room occupied by the leaches, furnaces, and entrance to the machinery and sweat-rooms is about 27 feet lengthwise in the tannery, and the full width, which is 40 feet. *H* is 2 copper heaters (placed in the bottom of the leachers), each 3 feet in diameter and 15 feet long, tapering off at one end to 12 inches in diameter; the 12-inch pipe runs four times through the leaches, and enters a stock about 18 inches

involves a consideration of much importance.

Seventh, Is it reasonable to suppose that it requires from one to seven years, as we are told it formerly did in England, to make leather from hides, when the same work can be accomplished in the space of three months?

But persons unacquainted with the nature and principles of tanning generally suppose that the longer time skins are undergoing the process of tanning the better will be the quality of the leather produced. This is a great mistake. But how did this opinion gain

---

below the top of the leach, making each heater 75 feet in length, including the small and large portion; each heater runs through two leaches. *J* and *V* is the mouth of the furnace in the heaters, where fuel enters and heat is obtained for heating the leaches. *I* is the stock or chimney, to which the heaters are connected, for discharging smoke and gas from the furnace. *K* is a hide-mill or fulling stock (for a full description see Chapter IV). *W* is a washing-machine (for particulars see Chapter IV., page 49). *Y* is 3 pools for soaking dry hides; each pool is 9

credence and become so general? By (in my opinion) tanners, who do not understand the first principles of their calling, attempting to tan quickly by applying strong liquors, at first, to hides not properly cleansed and prepared in the beam-house for the liquors, and by a neglect of handling, or a proper degree of agitation while the process is going on. If you want to tan quickly, and produce good and heavy leather, have your skins properly prepared in the beam-house. This is the grand starting-point in the manufacture of good leather, and much more depends upon this

---

feet long, 5 feet wide, and 6 feet deep,--which will hold 810 cubic feet of water; this soak and wash-room occupies 18 feet by 40. *L* is the beam-house; the portion used for unhairing and bating the hides is 48 feet in length and 40 feet in width, making the beam-house, soak and wash-room 66 feet in length and 40 feet wide. *M* is 6 vats, 9 feet long, 6 feet wide, and 6 feet deep,—for liming and bating purposes. *N* is 4 vats or pools, 8 feet long, 7 feet wide, and 6 feet deep,—used for the purpose of washing and rinsing the hides. *X* is a trap-door, to hoist the

branch of the manufacture than most tanners suppose. If for limed stock, either for upper or sole-leather, have your hides in good order for the lime,—that is, soft enough, but not too soft, for dried skins may be very much injured by being softened too much. (A hide, when just taken from the animal, should be the criterion; it is then best suited for the lime.) Then put them in the lime, and have them frequently agitated, and keep them in no longer than will be sufficient to loosen the hair that it may be removed. After the hair is completely removed, the skins are washed

---

stock up into the upper stories by means of a pulley or a hoisting tackle. *Q* is the handling-house, 26 feet long and 40 feet wide (see description in Chapter X). *P* is 2 pumps, for pumping the liquors from the junks, which are each 10 feet square and 12 feet deep; when full, will hold 2,400 cubic feet of tanning liquor. *S* is 8 handlers, 3 of which are 7 feet in width, 8 feet in length, and 6 feet in depth; the 5 on the opposite side are 4 feet wide, 8 feet long, and 6 feet deep; these vats are used for the first introduction of skins to the tanning ooze. *U* is 68 tan

in a vat full of water, and are then subjected to a weak liquor at first, which must be gradually strengthened until the stock is completely tanned.

Leather is an article of universal use. It is worn by the civilized and by the savage, the high and the low, the rich and the poor of all nations, from the icy regions of the north to the burning sands of the tropic. It was known and used by man long before the first alphabet was invented—before the waters of the deluge had rolled over the face of our planet—before the Tower of Babel was

---

vats,—24 of which are 8 feet in length, 7 feet in width, and 5½ feet in depth; the balance, being 44 vats, are 7½ feet long, 3½ feet wide, and 5½ feet deep. *O* is the doors for passing in and out the tannery. *R* is a railroad, of 2½ feet track, running through the center of the tannery, running from the bark-room down through the center, and out at the lower end, and around to the bank of the river, for carrying out the waste materials and carrying the stock through the different parts of the factory; and also a railroad running across in front of the furnaces, and out at

erected—or the foundations of the ever-enduring Pyramids were laid.

Leather is an article of manufacture,—entirely a compound substance, a chemical product. Although it is made of the skins of animals, it is as different from the raw material as oil—one of its two ingredients—is from soap. Skins are principally composed of gelatin, which is soluble in hot water, and is converted into glue by repeated steepings in warm water. Leather is simply the raw material combined with other substances, which render it elastic and insoluble in water. Various substances

---

each side, down on the lower side to the wood and coal-yard, and, on the upper side, across the turnpike to the storehouse. This latter road is for carrying hides from the warehouse into the tannery, and the leather into the warehouse, and also for bringing fuel into the factory for heating purposes. The second story of the building is occupied for finishing purposes, and is furnished with a railroad, running through the center from one end to the other, for the convenience of the workmen. The third story is used for drying the stock, which is also possessed

are employed to obtain this result; and different qualities of leather are produced by the different ingredients employed and the modes of using them in its manufacture.

The process of manufacture is named tanning, and the principal substance employed is tannic acid. This acid is found in various substances. Good upper-leather should have the following qualities,—elasticity, softness, and insolubility in water. Good sole-leather should be close in the grain, firm, but slightly elastic, and perfectly water-proof. Tannic acid is extracted from various sub-

---

with the convenience of a railroad. The bark-shed, on the north end of the factory, is 90 feet long, 40 feet wide, and 16 feet high, with a railroad in the center, running from the upper or north end down to the bark-mill. The floor of the shed is on a level with the floor in the second story of the tannery. The shed will hold, when full, 450 cords of bark, besides other sheds of similar size, within one and three hundred yards distant from the factory, but connected by railroad.

This commodious edifice is situated on the east bank of

stances containing tannin, by immersing those ingredients in hot water, and thereby forming a decoction of tanning ooze. By simply steeping the hides in this tan-liquor, the tannin leaves the water, combines with the gelatine of the skin chemically, and forms our "understandings," which we term Leather. This is the theory of tanning; but, in carrying it into practice, the manipulations are exceedingly various, and the qualities of the leather manufactured depend on a very extensive range of processes, machinery, and chemical substances. All the processes of tanning are laborious, expensive,

---

the Schuylkill River, about 1½ miles from Clinton Village, which is situated on the west side of the river, nearly opposite the tannery. The factory is about one mile from the Kittanning or Blue Mountains, where bark is obtained in an abundance at a very small cost, and is used in connection with my chemicals. The main road or turnpike from Pottsville to Reading is about 20 yards distant, and parallel with the front of the tannery. On the same level, about 100 yards from the tannery, is a storehouse, 20 feet by 50, and 2 stories high. On the same side of the road,

and tedious. It formerly required months and years to tan leather from hides; and the cost of manufacturing leather from the raw material amounted to millions of dollars annually; but now time and expense are materially reduced.

Inventive genius has done wonders in facilitating chemico-physical processes of this art. Only think for a moment of the change which has come over the spirit of the tanner's dream. Three, and even seven years, were once considered necessary for the perfection of certain kinds of leather,—such as that which furnishes our shoe-soles. The machinery-

---

a short distance above the storehouse, are about 20 dwelling houses, and also a fine, commodious hotel, and several mechanical shops. This commodious factory, and all the convenience of water power, and facilities of shipping hides and leather, are represented by a wood engraving in front of this chapter. About 400 yards from the north end of the tannery—which is seen on the engraving—is a bridge, built across the Schuylkill River, through which is a road leading up to Clinton, which is also seen in a distant view from the factory. About 300 yards from the

aided process by which these wonders have been accomplished, has been known and used in this country for some years.

By the aid of this new process, whose principle is to bring the skins into rapidly-repeated contact with the tanning liquor, leather is formed more rapidly and expeditiously, and of a better quality. But no important improvement in any manufacturing business can come into general use without the co-operation of energetic business men engaged in it.

In this age of improvements it cannot

---

tannery is a dam, built across the river, 30 feet high, by the Schuylkill Navigation Company, for the use of their canal. A little above the dam is a race, made for the purpose of supplying the factory with water, affording a very extensive power to turn the different machinery or works in the tannery; and also a tail-race or waste-way, for carrying the waste water from the factory into the river. On the opposite side of the river from the tannery, between the river and Clinton Village, is a canal, or the Schuylkill Navigation; and between the canal and the village is seen

possibly be considered a fixed fact that everything has arrived at its "manifest destiny" of perfection. There is room for improvements in every branch of manufacturing business. As to the art of tanning, I consider it yet in its infancy.

The only way to progress is to make efforts to improve; and the failure of a thousand plans should never be held up as a bugbear, or a barrier to arrest the introduction and trial of a new and reasonable process to improve any art. It is my opinion that improvements will

---

on the engraving the Reading Railroad, running from Philadelphia to Reading and Pottsville. The railroad depot is also represented by the engraving, which is one mile from the tannery.

This large leather factory, referred to in the illustration, was constructed upon my improved plan, and produces double the amount of tanned leather in one year than any other tannery in the State of the same size and expense. This factory is tanning about 15,000 sides a year, besides a great number of small skins. At the Clinton Tannery

yet be made in the manufacture of leather of such a character as will reduce its manufacturing cost at least one-half.

After several years' experimenting in the tanning of leather, and in trying to facilitate and expedite the process of manufacturing it,—I was very successful. However, experimenting with a variety of materials is very tedious, laborious, and expensive. In a pursuit of this kind the patience of Job is often required. Attempts at improvement, perseveringly repeated, will in the end seldom fail.

---

the greatest strength of liquors used for handling, as indicated by Pike's barkometer, is 13 degrees; that employed in laying away varies from 35 to 50 degrees. Much care and judgment is necessary in proportioning the continually increasing strength of the liquors to the requirements of the leather in different stages of the process. A glance at the illustration, and also at these notes, will at once convince any one that the advantages of such an establishment can not be surpassed by any other in the States.

THE COAT-OF-ARMS OF THE UNITED STATES.

CHAPTER XV.

THE MECHANIC'S TRUE POSITION.

In passing through our land and observing the young, the eager, and the intelligent who are destined hereafter to fill high posts of trust and honor,—that from these would come your princely merchants, your aldermen, mayors, representatives, men of iron nerves, warm hearts, and clear heads, ready to compete for the highest places in the pulpit, at the bar, or on the forum, and even, perhaps, the highest office in the gift of a free people,—why may they not rank, by their industry, intelligence, and virtue, among those whom America will be proud to number among her devoted

TRUE SON OF AMERICA.

and patriotic sons? Not for ourselves alone is the grand law of Nature inscribed on all the Creator's works,—not for ourselves alone, but for others, does the sun dispense his beams,—not for ourselves alone do the clouds distil their showers nor the teeming earth unlock her treasures! So, my brother mechanics, it is not for ourselves alone, but for others, and for all, that the blessings of heaven are so plentifully bestowed upon man. All that any of us can say is, that we are the almoners of God's bounty, and that what constitutes the true wealth of this great country—it is labor! Fix it as you will—let who will live upon our bread and meat—still, labor lies at the foundation of all, and, without it, neither society nor civilization could exist. He who derides labor, or undervalues it, strikes at the order of Nature, the foundations of society—at civilization, and at Christianity itself. Labor is the very Gold of Ophir—the true, intrinsic wealth of a nation. The gold of eloquence or the silver of rhetoric I have none, but such as I have give I unto you.

THE FARMER PLOWING.

The hardy tillers of the soil are the foundation, and our industrious, working mechanics, the builders of our mighty fabric of national wealth, independence, and happiness. The laboring men and mechanics of our country are the true bone and sinew of the land—the main-spring and support of the machine of government. They are, in truth, the creators of a nation's wealth—the great artificers of national prosperity. If the tyrant, Louis XIV., in the glory of his most splendid reign, could utter, in the pride of his borrowed royalty, the sentence, "I am the State," with how much more truth can we, the working men of the nation, say—and how much more noble and true does it sound when we, the people, say—"We are the State?" Where the mechanics are down-trodden and depressed—made hewers of wood and drawers of water to those who have robbed them of their rights—there, such a monster as Louis, and other crowned heads, might well say, "I am the State." But let labor be honored as it is here—let light be shed upon the great depths of despotism as we now see it beginning to beam in Europe—and you will see the people there, as here, rising in their majesty and saying to their banished monarchs, "We are the State." Let there be no more kings nor queens! The mechanic is not only the architect and builder of his own fortune, of society's and of a nation's prosperity, but his is one of the most independent classes in the community. The professional man depends upon his mental gifts or acquirements; and when he fails to gain the popular favor, or, by some sudden change, loses it, he is put to desperate shifts to earn a livelihood. You have seen the crest-fallen lawyer, or the proud statesman or politician, humbly suing for aid at the comfortable fire-side of the mechanic. The skillful artisan is an independent man; for, place him in whatever part of the world you may, he can always secure his bread, because he is capable of doing something that is useful to his fellow-man. The story of the two men cast away among savages is an apt illustration. One was a gentleman, the other a basket-maker; the basket-maker was well treated because he could do something for himself; but the savages, in their simplicity, could not understand what a gentleman is, and the basket-maker's handiwork saved the poor gentleman from starving. In the circles where true refinement never dwells, you may hear the expression sometimes used, as if in derision or commiseration, "O, he is only a working mechanic!" It may seem strange, but there are men, and women, too, who can boast no other lineage themselves, and who, when told of this poor man's misfortune, or that man's sudden fall, pass over the matter with the cold remark of, "He is only a mechanic!" There are more happy, prosperous, noble men among the laboring mechanics of this, our land, than in any other class of equal numbers. There was a certain man, called Felix, in the Scriptures; his countrymen were a proud race, and hated the laboring mechanic; but one of these despised men—a tent-maker—made this same Felix tremble, although only a mechanic. Noah was a shipwright; Solomon an architect; and those who built the pyramids, and planned the ancient cities, whose ruins all the historians, philosophers, and learned men of modern times are yet unable fully to explain,—the great temples of the holy city of Jerusalem,—the renowned structures of Tyre and Sidon, of Balbec and Persepolis, of Babylon and Palmyra, Thebes and Memphis,—wondrous monuments of the East, whose magnificence no modern art can excel,—who built them? O, it was only mechanics! And then, who was the first mechanic? The great Author of our being, that first built the world; and then, as the sublimity of mechanism, He made us "fearfully and wonderfully." Give your attention for a moment to the impulse given to modern improvement and the change wrought upon the face of the whole world by the invention of Faust, who gave light and knowledge to all mankind. To the discoveries of Columbus, the science of

BENJAMIN FRANKLIN SETTING TYPE.

Franklin, the ingenuity of Arkwright, the genius of Fulton and of Whitney,—mechanics all,—what does this nation owe?—what does the civilized world owe, to these great men? All the improvements that were ever made by all the kings and emperors, and by all the artists, poets, philosophers, and statesmen that ever lived, you may pile up in one scale, and they are outweighed by the discoveries of Faust, Fulton, and Whitney; and yet these men earned their bread by the sweat of their brow! We have a right to be proud that Franklin, and Fulton, and Whitney were all countrymen of ours, although only mechanics. Young as we are as a nation, such is the free scope and tendency of our institutions, and the salubrity of our glorious climate, to foster the full energies of the mind and to produce the whole man, that, in all the useful mechanic arts, we are outstripping the nations of the old world. In arts, and in arms, and in every worldly pursuit of man, our advancement stands unequaled since the world began. You all have duties to perform as citizens, neighbors, members of the great community of working and active men. Rome was not built in a day; nor can anything great or noble in human ingenuity be accomplished without labor. It is the boast of the workingman that he can do what he says. The mechanics of our country, active and intelligent as they are, may proudly hold up their heads, as a body, and say boldly to the politicians and the orators of the day, "What you promise we perform." While making some observations on this glorious republic, destined to be the greatest in the world, for evidences not only of what mechanics can do, but what they have done, go into your public edifices, your exchanges, your temples devoted to the worship of God, and your halls of education, and there you will see the handiwork of labor. Look into your banks, your city councils, and then abroad into your States, and the most successful, the most illustrious and beloved, are the ones who early learned the lesson of labor and how to think for themselves; they were always up to their business, but never above it.

There are two great levers which sustain us,—the one is employment; the other, the knowledge of how to regulate and improve it. In other words, they are the union of occupation and instruction. Nothing can give more satisfaction to the mind than the enjoyment of the necessaries and comforts of life flowing from the industry of him who earns them. This is the fruit of occupation; and the improvements of society follow in proportion as the occupied mind advances in proper cultivation. The absurd idea, that labor is inconsistent with learning or respectability, is one of the errors of weak minds, ignorant of the nature of the ligaments which bind society together. It is one of the follies of antiquated fashion which is passing away; and we are now beginning to consider the mechanic trades, and all branches of honest industry, as the co-ordinate and necessary associates of education, integrity and manliness. The history of the social operations of mankind teaches us that, in all periods of time, they have altered the destinies of individuals as well as of nations, and have had their influence upon ages to come. The physical industry of man is certainly a high quality; but, vigorous as it is, it gains so much by its association with a cultivated intellect, that while the one, when alone, resembles the rough materials of handicraft, and the other the latent genius that is to fashion them, they, both united, represent the perfection of skill and its fruitful application to the production of human happiness. In former days, trades were merely physical; none of the sciences, and but few branches of the fine arts, entered into their action. True, there were some few exceptions, dependent upon individual condition and scholarship; but, generally, labor in any calling was strictly and exclusively mechanical. There is now, however, a progressive spirit which belongs to the times. Whether it has resulted from the institutions of this country—which, by casting off the trammels of political tyranny, and by the abundance of our land for an easy support, have enabled men to think more freely and consistently with the object of their creation and position—or is a part of a pervading principle which the Divine Being has permitted to spread through the world, is a problem for solution. Be this as it may, we see that there is evidently an advance in the different trades and their branches, a more intimate relationship between mind and the labors of the operator, a clearer working through the lights of reason, so that, even among the inferior callings, the lamp of science sheds its rays, even if it is seen only in flickerings from the distance at which it stands. It has been said that all men have their mental affinities; that some pass unheeded away, without having left any "footprints in the sand of time," only because the period of their sojourning presented no occasions, no elective influence to draw out their energies or their talents, while the great are but the creatures of opportunity, or who, having been touched by the Ithuriel wand, have sprung out into light, brightness, and renown. Opportunity is certainly a great ingredient in any effort; and without it, either offered or acquired, no voluntary act can well succeed.' The tanner should have a thorough knowledge of chemistry; and, by applying his acquired knowledge to the branch of industry which has engaged his special attention, he makes a good leather manufacturer and becomes a well-instructed man in the general business of life. The characteristic traits of a man are also elements of his future; but still it should add to the credit of the individual, who, cultivating an understanding of his nature and his latent abilities, uses them to advantage in that "tide in the affairs of men, which, taken at the flood, leads on to fortune." The time was, and in some degree still is, when reputation in honors was principally founded upon, and esteemed for, distinction in literature, the fine arts, the emblazonments of wealth, and the positions which they respectively gave. The rest, like hewers of wood and drawers of water who served at the building of Solomon's temple, were supposed to be sufficiently compensated by the daily penny paid for their labors. No mark or memorial was left upon the edifice of their works; and, except in the narrow circle of their industry, none knew of their labors or their zeal. In the general operations of the society of the good and hardy tanners, it is not to be expected that the mere ordinary components of that great whole shall be held in any special remembrance, either in the present or the future. Much will be, as has already been, done by the agency of those very qualities in placing honorable occupation of labor upon the true level of its merits. Tanner, pause, and accompany me, for a moment, to what has already been observed relative to labor and industry; mark out the way, and forget not to follow it.

The end crowns the work, and so have the good results of labor left a crown upon the name more endearing to the good man than all the pomp and circumstance that power, alone, or wealth could purchase. The days of chivalry arising from the power of kings and nobles, the empires of war and victories, crusades of faith, and the necessary maintenance of the followers of such errantries, as well while they lasted as in "the cankers of a long peace," were the beginnings of the false distinctions which made idleness honorable and left industry with only the reward of its own products. It takes time to accomplish any revolution which shall be of permanent benefit; and it is proper it should be so, as improvements are worked out in the progress of experience which could not be made in a leap from one condition to another. The doctrine of a necessity for useful occupation in all men is a great element in this change. Men do not begin to think calmly or wisely in the turmoil of exciting pursuits. It is only when they are falling into their proper places in the great community, and putting their shoulder to the wheel to do something useful, that they perceive their relative positions, their obligations, and the duties which belong to them as integrants of the whole. It is, therefore, industry which is the groundwork of reform, both moral and political; it is the basis of domestic virtue, comfort, and plenty; and the producer of what sustains a nation and improves its condition. When to this is added education, its followers are the supporters of man in all his conditions, wants, advances, and elegancies of life, and are the safeguards of society.

These reflections arise spontaneously from the nature of the subject we are discussing, as being intimately connected with the career of the good man, reclaiming or saving from time what would otherwise be lost. If it be creditable to perpetuate the knowledge of the deeds of man in arms—of wars that have desolated the earth and left misery and sighs to be felt again in after ages by those who deprecate and sympathize while they read—how much more worthy an effort is it to record in imperishable form the good civic conduct of those unpretending men who have labored during their lives for the common weal, and who make, in every field, two blades of grass grow where only one grew before?

In the world's broad field of battle—
  In the bivouac of life—
Be not like the driven cattle;
  Be a hero in the strife!

Lives of great men all remind us,
  We can make our own sublime,
And, departing, leave behind us
  Footsteps in the sand of time.

Let us, then, be up and doing,
  With a heart for any fate;
Still achieving, still pursuing,
  Learn to labor and to wait.

* * * * * * *

It belongs to you, my brother mechanic, to rise in the world. You who are willing to be advised by those who have experience, consult the wise and good and profit by their examples. If you would succeed in life, let your motto be not only to look ahead, but go ahead. Set your mark high, and strive to reach it. You can succeed if you will remember, my friends, the almost omnipotent power of perseverance, the power of industry and of labor—you who are just beginning the world—that fourteen or sixteen hours a day are sure to foot a good account and seldom need an indorser. "Order is heaven's first law," and the Scripture tells us to "Let everything be done decently and in order." The man of method is generally a successful man. The neglect of this great principle has ruined its tens of thousands. An excellent rule is, Let nothing be neglected that can be done to-day. Whatever you undertake, pursue it steadily if you wish to succeed; for wherever there is a will there is a way; then forget not the advice of the wise man, "And with all thy getting get understanding." Bear in mind that the laboring mechanic should educate his head, his hands, and his heart. He will thus learn to distinguish good from evil, to know how to supply his wants and add to his comforts, and how to dispense blessings to all around him.

TANNERS SINGING THE "TANNERS' CHEER," ADAPTED TO THE TUNE OF THE MARSEILLAISE HYMN.

CHAPTER XVI.

THE TANNERS' CHEER.

Award of cheer to the hearty tanner,
  And a blessing on his trade;
A leather bough shall be his banner,
  Over all the land displayed.

Amid the forest-giant's winding,
  While far away the hunter's coil
Round the wild bull's neck is binding,
  He marks the noblest for his spoil.

Work on, ye Pitmen all!
  And let the hide be sound
Work on! joy to the land
  Where working-men abounc

His labor gives the world protection
  In an ever changing form,
From the summer sun's reflection
  And the winter's raging storm.

It guards the tread of the sturdy yeoman,
  And guides his plow-horse over the mead;
It adorns the lovely foot of woman,
  And reins the patriot's battle steed.

Work on, ye Curriers all!
  And let the beam resound;
Work on! joy to the land
  Where working-men abound!

The wit and lore of bygone ages,
  His labor saves from swift decay;
It guards the Bible's holy pages,
  And grasps the follies of the day.

It aids the loom's bright imitation
  By turning every busy wheel;
It bears the stream to stay the conflagration,
  And sheathes the warrior's flashing steel.

Work on, ye Tanners all!
  And let the song go round;
Work on! joy to the land
  Where working-men abound!

See illustration in front of this chapter, representing a party of Tanners singing the above words.

FRONT VIEW OF THE UNITED STATES PATENT OFFICE, WASHINGTON, D. C.

CHAPTER XVII.

COPY OF PATENT, GRANTED APRIL 14, 1857.

THE UNITED STATES OF AMERICA.

TO ALL TO WHOM THESE LETTERS PATENT SHALL COME:

WHEREAS, David H. Kennedy, of New Alexandria, Pennsylvania, has alleged that he has invented a new and useful composition for tanning hides, which he states has not been known or used before his application; has made oath that he is a citizen of the United States; that he does verily believe that he is the original and first inventor or discoverer of the said composition, and that the same hath not, to the best of his knowledge and belief, been previously known or used, has paid into the treasury of the UNITED STATES the sum of thirty dollars, and presented a petition to the COMMISSIONER OF PATENTS, signifying a desire of obtaining an exclusive property in the said composition, and praying that a patent may be granted for that purpose,—

THESE ARE, THEREFORE, to grant, according to law, to the said David H. Kennedy, his heirs, administrators, or assigns, for the term of fourteen years, from the fourteenth day of April, one thousand eight hundred and fifty-seven, the full and exclusive right and liberty of making, constructing, using, and vending to others to be used, the said composition, a description whereof is given in the words of the said Kennedy, in the schedule hereunto annexed, and is made a part of these presents.

In testimony whereof, I have caused these letters to be made patent, and the seal of the PATENT OFFICE has been hereunto affixed. GIVEN under my hand, at the city of Washington, this fourteenth day of April, in the year of our Lord one thousand eight hundred and fifty-seven, and of the INDEPENDENCE of the United States of America the eighty-first.

JACOB THOMPSON,
Secretary of the Interior.

[L. S.] S. T. SHUGERT,
Asst. Comm'r of Patents.

Countersigned, and sealed with the seal of the Patent Office.

CHAPTER XVIII.

COPY OF SPECIFICATION OF PATENT.

THE SCHEDULE REFERRED TO IN THESE LETTERS PATENT, AND MAKING PART OF THE SAME.

To all to whom these presents shall come:

Be it known that I, David H. Kennedy, formerly of Reading, in the county of Berks, but now of New Alexandria, in the county of Westmoreland, and State of Pennsylvania, have invented or discovered certain new and useful compositions of matter to be used in the tanning of leather; and the following is a full, clear, and exact description of the manner of preparing and using the same:

This composition consists of .... pounds of .... or of ... .; ..... pounds of .... of ....; .... pounds of .... of .... or .... of ......; ... pound of .... of ....; ... pounds of ... . (......... of ....); ... pound of ..... or ....;

These ingredients should be dissolved separately in hot water, or in a hot decoction of tan bark, which is preferable, and then poured into a tank, and thoroughly stirred together to form the tanning liquor, which may be drawn off as required, to supply the vats or vessels in which the hides are to be tanned.

The tanning liquor thus formed in the tank is in the most concentrated form, and only suitable to apply to hides in the advanced stages of the tanning process, and must be largely diluted with water or bark-water before it is applied to hides at the commencement of this process; or else, before applying it to such hides, it should be partially spent by having had hides in a more advanced state steeped in it.

The strength of the liquor should be increased as the tanning progresses,—care being taken to handle the hides frequently in the early part of the process, while the liquor is weak; but less handling will do as the process advances. Hides intended for sole-leather may (near the close of the process) be laid down in a vat, alternately with layers of ground bark, and then a liquor, composed of three parts of the composition before mentioned and one part of strong bark liquor, should be poured into the vat until it covers the hides. Hides thus laid down may continue undisturbed until fully tanned—say from ten to fifteen days. Light skins need not be laid down, as they will be thoroughly tanned by merely handling in the liquor.

Hides will be tanned by this process quickly or slowly, according to the amount of handling and the strength of the tanning liquor. When a tan-yard has become impregnated thoroughly with the chemicals employed, the tanning will be performed with less expense than at first, the quality of the leather will be noticeably improved, and the time required for tanning diminished.

When the before mentioned tanning compound is employed with hemlock bark, in the proportion of fifteen pounds of the compound to about one hundred and twenty-eight cubic feet of the bark, the leather produced will have the color, pliancy, and other desirable qualities of the best oak-tanned leather. In this way the expense of oak-tanned leather will be greatly reduced, while the quality will be fully maintained.

What I claim as my invention, and desire to secure by LETTERS PATENT, is the combination of ...., the .... of ...., ... of ...., or .... of ......, and .... of ...., ...; ...., ... or ...., ..., dissolved in water or tan-bark liquor, for the purpose of tanning *hides* and *skins* substantially as herein set forth.

In testimony whereof I have hereunto subscribed my name.

DAVID H. KENNEDY.

DAVID BEDFORD,
JAMES B. DUNN, } Witnesses.

INDEX.

PAGE.

www.ingramcontent.com/pod-product-compliance
Lightning Source LLC
LaVergne TN
LVHW010243110826
845151LV00004B/1374

9781425523657